Church Educational Ministries

EVANGELICAL TEACHER TRAINING ASSOCIATION

110 Bridge Street, Box 327
Wheaton, Illinois 60187

Courses in the Advanced Certificate Program
> *The Missionary Enterprise*
> *Evangelize Thru Christian Education*
> *The Triune God*
> *Biblical Beliefs*
> *Church Educational Ministries or Vacation Bible School*
> *Your Bible*

Second Edition
Second Printing 1977

ISBN 0-910566-13-5

Library of Congress catalog card number: 67-27288

Copyright © 1968 by Evangelical Teacher Training Association

Printed in U.S.A.

Cover art and sketches by Richard W. Mlodock
Credit for photographs as follows: Christian Life Publications—pp. 7, 38, 46, 82; David C. Cook Foundation—p. 68; National Sunday School Association—p. 90; H. Armstrong Roberts—p. 15; Scripture Press Foundation—pp. 22, 30, 54, 60, 75.

PREFACE

Evangelical Teacher Training Association presents this text to provide a needed, practical overview of current Christian education activities. Prepared primarily for use as the text for a new E.T.T.A. Certificate study, *Church Educational Ministries* is a helpful book for all who are interested in Christian education.

The writer of each chapter is an experienced Christian educator. Each is well qualified in his subject and either has taught or is teaching in one of the schools holding membership in Evangelical Teacher Training Association. Since its founding, the Association has continued to contribute to advancing Christian education through relating schools of higher education to local church educational ministry.

Readers will find the guide questions at the beginning of each chapter helpful. Teachers will find the closing discussion questions valuable in their teaching, and all who wish to study any subject further will discover in the annotated bibliographies a wealth of supplemental material.

When used as part of the program of E.T.T.A. leadership preparation, this book will prove a practical textbook. As Christian education resource material or as a survey of church education potential, it can be read with profit by all church leaders.

> PAUL E. LOTH, ED.D., *President*
> *Evangelical Teacher Training Association*

ABOUT THIS BOOK

Books, like people, often benefit by a few words of introduction.

This is not simply a listing of educational programs. It is actually a study in *opportunities*—Christian education opportunities for the church to consider in the fulfilling of its ministry.

Not every church will use every program. But every church worker will profit by being acquainted with each and knowing its potential ministry in his church.

Although the text has been written by varied authors, each chapter has a basic pattern. This is not a study in depth, but the basics are here, as well as resource listings for further study.

Finally, the underlying premise of this text is that each activity presented finds its primary focus in the Gospel —the biblical message of new, and potentially full, life in Jesus Christ. When viewed and used in this perspective, the programs to be studied become in the fullest sense opportunities for productive ministry for our Lord in today's world!

WERNER C. GRAENDORF, Ph.D.

TABLE OF CONTENTS

Preface 3

About This Book 4

I. Church Education 7
DONALD J. TROUTEN, PH.D.

II. Church and Home 15
MORRIS A. INCH, PH.D.

III. The Sunday School 22
ANNA RIEGER, D.R.E.

IV. Weekday Bible Classes 30
RUTH C. HAYCOCK, ED.D.

V. Vacation Bible School 38
GENE GETZ, PH.D.

VI. Church Camping 46
PAUL R. FINK, TH.D.

VII. Adult Fellowship 54
ROBERT CLARK, ED.D.

VIII. Youth Program 60
GILBERT A. PETERSON, PH.D.

IX. Boys' and Girls' Clubs 68
J. OMAR BRUBAKER, M.A.

X. Children's Church 75
ROBERT F. RAMEY, TH.M.

XI. Missionary Education 82
F. IONE ANDERSON, M.A.

XII. The Board of Christian Education 90
EDWARD L. HAYES, PH.D.

CHAPTER 1

Church Education

DONALD J. TROUTEN

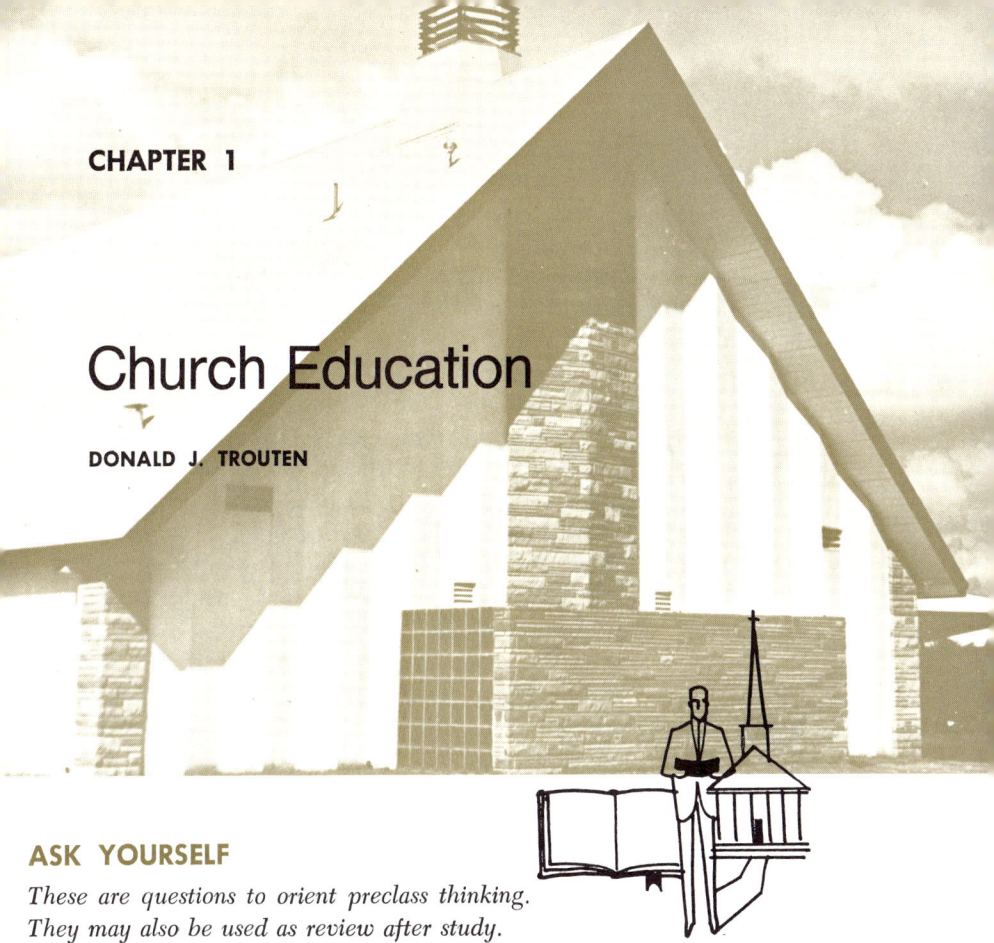

ASK YOURSELF

*These are questions to orient preclass thinking.
They may also be used as review after study.*

1. What distinguishes Christian education from education in general?
2. Why is it important for the church to have an educational ministry?
3. What was Christ's attitude toward teaching?
4. What is the relationship of Christian education to the total church program?
5. What are some objectives of Christian education?
6. What is the place of educational agencies other than the Sunday school in a church ministry?

DO YOU KNOW?

Christian education offers the evangelical church one of its greatest means for enlarged Gospel witness! New and challenging educational ministries, as well as established programs, are available for the church to use. In a day of steadily increasing secular influence, the alert church worker will want to be aware of all his opportunities.

Donald J. Trouten, Ph.D., *St. Paul Bible College faculty*

Basic, of course, to any study of church educational ministries, or agencies, is a good understanding of what is meant by Christian education. What are its purposes? What is its place in the church program?

An understanding of this type will give a practical foundation on which to discuss the educational agencies, as well as provide a sound framework within which to relate them to local church situations.

Christian education as a teaching ministry is not new in church work. It has been at the center of the church from the beginning of the Christian fellowship. It was Christ's commission to His disciples in Matthew 28, and it found expression in the writings and practices of the early church. During the dark periods of the Middle Ages it provided hope. Later an educational emphasis was dominant in the Protestant Reformation.

In America, Christian education and secular education were at one time virtually synonymous terms. Today, however, Christian influence in America is steadily decreasing. Recent Supreme Court decisions have affected religious influence through the public schools, and in very few homes is there family reading and study of Scriptures.

The public school cannot give religious education. The home is neglecting its responsibility for Christian teaching. It is indeed imperative for the church to use every opportunity and means for communicating the Gospel, and Christian education is an increasingly vital and opportune subject for study.

CHRISTIAN EDUCATION

What Is Christian Education?

Christian education is the communication of the Gospel through formal and informal educational programs so that the facts of Scripture are presented clearly and individuals respond by personal faith in Christ and by growth toward spiritual maturity.

Education has been defined as the discipline of mind or character through study or instruction. This applies also to Christian education. However, "Christian education" is a more definitive term than "education," for it involves specifically the Gospel message.

One educator defines Christian education as a process by which persons are confronted with and controlled by the Christian Gospel.

VALUES OF A CHURCH EDUCATIONAL PROGRAM

Honors Christ's Command

The church must teach, for our Lord said, "Go ye therefore and teach all nations . . . teaching them to observe all things whatsoever I have commanded you." Throughout His earthly ministry He Himself was an outstanding example of educator. His followers, as clearly shown in the book of Acts and the other New Testament writings, followed His command and example. Education is still our challenge, and Christian education is the responsibility of the entire church, not just of those who do the actual teaching of the Word of God.

Provides Evangelistic Outreach

The church in teaching presents the full message of the Gospel. At the very heart of such message is the call for personal faith in Jesus Christ. Every Sunday school class, and every other church educational effort that is true to the Word of God, involves the message of salvation. It is said that the disciples "ceased not to teach and preach Jesus Christ" (Acts 5:42). The church must use every opportunity to present Christ, and such agencies as vacation Bible school, boys' and girls' clubs, and weekday classes offer fruitful community evangelism outreaches.

Strengthens the Believers

One of the vital concerns of Christian education is the growth of the believer. This must be provided for on the level of the child, youth, and adult. A full program of Christian education offers opportunities for growth through varied means. The graded Sunday school has a ministry of the Word for all. The various age-grouped agencies, such as adult organizations, youth groups, and children's churches, provide special means for spiritual development.

Builds the Church and Its Leadership

Adults are a vital part of any sound plan of Christian education. Yet, we must recognize that a large percentage of adults will be receptive to the teachings of the church because they have been receptive to such teachings during their childhood and adolescence. It has been estimated that three out of four people who come to know Christ are converted before they have left adolescence. Most who respond to the call to vocational Christian service respond during adolescence or before. And it is here that agencies related to missionary education have an especially practical ministry. For it is the church's ministry not only to "save from," but also to "send forth." Christian education has a crucial role in the development of Christian discipleship.

Establishes the Church in Its Beliefs and Practice

An important objective of Christian nurture is the desired outcome that believers understand the basic aspects of their own church, and that they have an intelligent concept of why they are Christians. Many Christians become perplexed when witnessing to others and discussing their belief, for they discover that a disproportionate percentage of their convictions is based upon acceptance rather than understanding.

Believers need to understand also the significance of the various activities and practices of the church. Why is an offering taken? What do the bread and the cup mean in the communion service? What is the significance of baptism? What do the hymns mean? These are all essential aspects of meaningful participation in the church fellowship, and a challenge to the teaching ministry.

Gives Parental Guidance

Adults need spiritual guidance and wisdom if they are to obey the injunction of Scripture to bring up their children "in the nurture and admonition of the Lord." An effective Christian education ministry provides opportunities for parents to grow in their ability to establish and maintain a Christian witness in the home. Certainly the home itself is a key educational agency, and it needs to be used as such.

Conserves Church Heritage

The Christian church has a rich heritage of God at work in the lives of men and women. Old Testament history, as well as church history in general, tells of spiritual awakenings and victories that accompanied study and application of the Scriptures. This heritage should serve as reminder and encouragement. Here again Christian education can minister as it teaches both the Scriptures and the accounts of how God has blessed through them.

RELATIONSHIP OF EDUCATIONAL MINISTRY TO OTHER CHURCH ACTIVITIES

To Preaching

The educational ministry of the church is closely related to the preaching ministry. Much teaching takes place in good preaching. Both preaching and Christian education are theological in foundation. It is essential that there be no conflict between the theology presented from the pulpit and the theology presented in the classroom. The teachings from the various ministries of the church must flow together. Woodruff in his *Basic Concepts of Teaching* has an illustration of the Mississippi River, noting that it is a mighty river rather than a collection of puddles, swamps, and meandering streams because all its tributaries flow eventually and entirely into the main stream.[1] Thus, preaching and teaching in the church have a common purpose that builds the "main stream" of church life.

To Administration

If the educational ministry is to be an integral part of the church program, there must be definite lines of administrative relationship. This begins with recognition of the central place of the pastor as minister of the total church program. Where there is a director of Christian education, specified areas of responsibility are given to him. A clear understanding should be established as to authority, procedures, and personal relationships among all staff personnel.

The interrelationships and correlation of the total church program with regard to Christian education are normally the responsibility of a board of Christian education. This is discussed in the final chapter of this text.

ORGANIZING CHRISTIAN EDUCATION

Personnel

While Christian education is related to every church member, specified leadership must organize, correlate, and give direction. This usually calls for a board of Christian education. The enlistment and training of leadership for the various agencies is a large and continuing task, greatly assisted by a plan of continuous leadership training. It is here that an established program with foundational courses in Bible and Christian education offers the church a practical means for accomplishing its leadership goals.

Program

ITS AIMS

Aims are essential to an effective Christian education ministry. We cannot evaluate the degree of our success if we have no concept of the objectives for which we are striving. Aims, as Eavey points out, give direction, make for orderly continuity, provide a basis for selection of materials and activities, give a sound basis for measurement, encourage right aims in pupils,

---

[1] Asahel D. Woodruff, *Basic Concepts of Teaching* (San Francisco: Chandler Publishing Company, 1961), pp. 43, 44.

and keep the teacher courageous and energetic.[2]

They have an essential place in the entire educational program:

> Education is planned around objectives ranging from one large major purpose for all education, down to the specific single objective of one lesson. The large purposes are approached by means of the small single lesson objectives . . . Learning moves cumulatively toward the major objective when each successive lesson presents one of these concepts or skills as its objective.[3]

Three major areas of aims should be noted for Christian education. These concern salvation, Christian growth, and preparation for service.

Personal faith in Christ is basic. "The foundational aim in Christian education is the bringing of the individual to Christ for salvation."[4] Involved in personal decisions, of course, is knowledge for decision and in this context each educational effort of the church is in itself a vital force for evangelism. This is emphasized by the large number of decisions for Christ made in later life which were based largely on teaching given in the earlier years.

The aim of Christian growth—bringing the believer to spiritual maturity—is also at the heart of Christian education. It associates application with knowledge. Thus, Christian growth, especially in terms of Christian conduct, becomes an important measure of the success of the Christian education effort.

A third goal of the educational work of the church should be preparation for service. We need to provide opportunity for believers to develop their abilities as servants of Christ. Likewise, we should include in our educational program opportunities at various levels for actual Christian service.

ITS SCOPE

The program of instruction in the local church has traditionally included the pulpit and the Sunday school class. These are important foundations in the Christian education program of most churches. But there are significant educational agencies beyond these, as presented and discussed in this text.

Even when the Sunday school is attended regularly, a relatively brief time of actual instruction is gained each week. However, the addition of a vacation Bible school program, for example, could add many hours of instruction. Weekday youth

---

[2] C. B. Eavey, *Principles of Teaching for Christian Teachers* (Grand Rapids: Zondervan Publishing House, 1940), pp. 47-51.
[3] Woodruff, *op. cit.*, p. 43.
[4] C. B. Eavey, "Aims and Objectives of Christian Education," *An Introduction to Evangelical Christian Education*, ed. J. Edward Hakes (Chicago: Moody Press, 1964), p. 62.

and children's activities add further outreach, and camping and conferences bring in another teaching dimension.

Not only is it a matter of increased teaching time, but just as important is the opportunity to reach individuals on a variety of age levels and areas of personal interest.

Equipment and Facilities

Good equipment and facilities are not to be equated with good education. However, they contribute greatly to it. The church that has satisfactory facilities and is well equipped greatly aids its teachers and workers in their educational ministry.

Each Sunday school class, for example, benefits by carefully selected teaching aids, proper height chairs and tables, and a chalkboard. A church library for class and teacher reference is likewise a valuable asset.

Financing

Regardless of a church's particular financial policy, the educational program should always be an important part of the budget planning. If the educational agencies are to be the church's ministry, they must also be related to the church's budget. Where there is a board of Christian education, one of its responsibilities is the Christian education budget. Adequate provision needs to be made for each agency to carry on its work as effectively as possible.

SUMMARY

The church as educator is responsible for Christian education. Increasingly such education must be given by the church if it is to be given at all.

The values of a church educational program center on reaching the individual with the Gospel and guiding him into Christian living. This involves children, youth, and adults in various aspects of church and home activities.

The relationship of the educational program to the total church ministry is of vital importance. The theology of the classroom, for example, must be in keeping with the theology of the pulpit. Similarly, there must be established lines of responsibility and close coordination.

Effective Christian education must also have aims. These relate to salvation, Christian growth, and Christian service. In carrying out its educational aims, the church will be concerned with using every possible means available to it, including the educational agencies presented in this textbook.

SHARING YOUR THINKING

1. Examine several instances in the New Testament where Christ is teaching or is referred to as a teacher, and discuss His methods of teaching.
2. Compare the teaching emphasis of Christ and Paul, using specific New Testament references.
3. Choose a Christian education objective and discuss how a particular church educational agency, other than the Sunday school, might help meet it.

PRACTICAL PROJECTS

1. List all of the organizations in your church involved in Christian education and chart their relationships to each other.
2. Collect examples of Christian influence, or lack of it, from current newspapers and magazines and relate to Christian education.
3. Prepare a list of Christian education objectives for your church, basing it on specific needs.

RESOURCES

Bibliography

Benson, Clarence. **The Sunday School in Action.** Chicago: Moody Press, 1941.
> Although an older book, Benson's work is valuable for general background material and insights.

Byrne, H. W. **Christian Education for the Local Church.** Grand Rapids: Zondervan Pub. House, 1963.
> Chapter 1 presents the purpose, pattern, and program of the church in Christian education with helpful clarifying charts.

Eavey, C. B. **History of Christian Education.** Chicago: Moody Press, 1964.
> An up-to-date study on the development of Christian education.

_____. **Principles of Teaching for Christian Teachers.** Grand Rapids: Zondervan Publishing House, 1940.
> A useful text on the basics of the teaching art.

Gaebelein, Frank E. **Christian Education in a Democracy.** New York: Oxford University Press, 1951.
> A significant book on the philosophy and practice of Christian education from an evangelical viewpoint.

Hakes, J. Edward (ed.). **An Introduction to Evangelical Christian Education.** Chicago: Moody Press, 1964.
> This book is a collection of chapters written by various authorities on 32 pertinent areas of Christian education.

Person, Peter P. **Introduction to Christian Education.** Grand Rapids: Baker Book House, 1958.
> A good book to introduce the reader to the scope of Christian education.

CHAPTER 2

Church and Home

MORRIS A. INCH

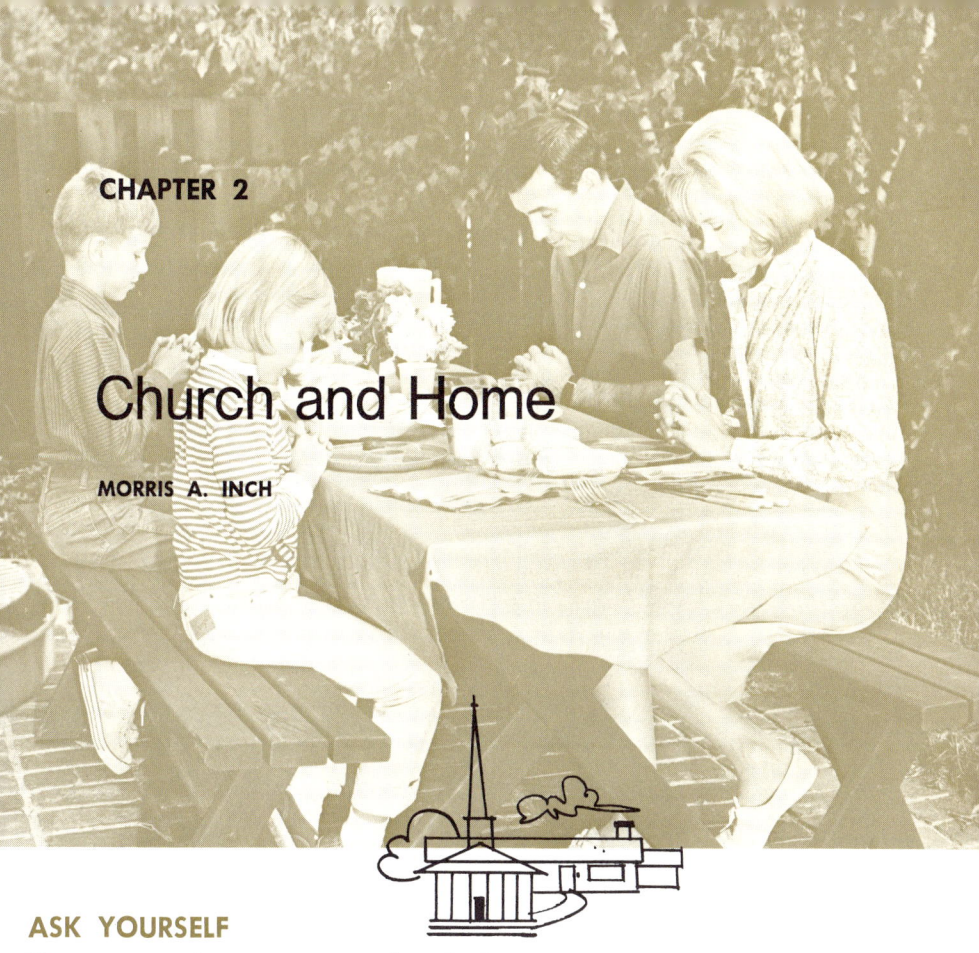

ASK YOURSELF

*These are questions to orient preclass thinking.
They may also be used as review after study.*

1. What is the place of the home in the church's educational program?
2. In what ways does the church strengthen the home?
3. In what areas can the church be of specific help to parents?
4. How might the church and home cooperate during the week?
5. What type of organization does church-home cooperation require?

DO YOU KNOW?

Church-home cooperation is an essential part of the church's educational ministry. "To face the stark realities of the breakdown of family life in America and to bolster the strength of genuine Christian family life, the church is faced with the responsibility of making provisions for Christian family education . . ."[1]

---

[1] H. W. Byrne, *Christian Education for the Local Church* (Grand Rapids: Zondervan Publishing House, 1963), p. 298.

Morris A. Inch, Ph. D., *Wheaton College faculty*

Church and home are both agencies charged by God with the responsibility of Christian education. In the Old Testament the home was the basic educational agency for Jewish society. The Apostle Paul reflected this in New Testament teaching as he wrote: "Ye fathers, provoke not your children to wrath: but bring them up in the nurture and admonition of the Lord" (Eph. 6:4).

On the other hand, home instruction has not precluded the need for gifted teachers to exercise special responsibility within the church.[2]

The home and the church have a joint ministry, and only as there is planned and enthusiastic cooperation between them can we expect Christian education to be fully effective.

What is Church-Home Educational Cooperation?

Church-home educational cooperation is the planned program of the church to assist and work with the home in communicating spiritual truths, by teaching and by example, to the whole family.

VALUES OF CHURCH-HOME COOPERATION

Cooperation between church and home results in benefits for both.

The church ministry is strengthened by the broadening of its base of operation and by the reenforcing of its teaching by home support.

Homes are helped by the church's recognition of the importance of the home, and by being able to draw on the church's resources.

In that the basic focus of both the church and the home is the individual believer, he gains directly as church teaching is implemented by home example and encouragement.

TYPES OF CHURCH-HOME COOPERATION

The Church Assisting the Home

The church works with the home by strengthening the spiritual life of family members; by providing information and counsel; and by demonstrating patterns for Christian living.

SPIRITUAL STRENGTHENING

The church and home may be separate teaching agencies, but the persons taught and the teaching responsibility are held in common. The church's activities strongly influence the

---

[2]Compare I Cor. 12:29; Eph. 4:11.

spiritual atmosphere of the home and the family fellowship. Family devotions, for example, can be greatly strengthened by the church's teaching and encouragement.

INFORMATION AND COUNSEL

The church serves as a resource guide for parents by providing specialized information and spiritual counsel. Such information or questions may pertain to the meaning of Scripture, church and denominational history and practice, or the application of Christian ideals to behavior and service.

Christian parents are sometimes poorly prepared to answer perplexing family questions. Many homes reflect the pattern of our society, rather than Christian standards. Here alert church-home cooperation can offer parents a practical resource for sound biblical guidance.

Professional counsel implies assistance either at some significant life juncture, or aid with certain problem areas. Crucial life events include marriage, birth of children, dedication and baptism, choice of vocation, serious illness, retirement, and death.

PATTERNS FOR LIVING

Paul enjoined: "Be of the same mind one toward another" (Rom. 12:16a). The church is a community under the law of God and alive by the Spirit of God. Love is to operate, teaching man how to relate to his fellow believer. Persons are to be accepted, encouraged, and committed to God in prayer, and barriers which separate are broken down in Christ. Here is a pattern for home life as Christian principles of human relationships are put into practice.

The Home Assisting the Church

The work of the church needs home support. It is difficult for a church to be effective in the application of Gospel truth without such support.

> The church cannot accomplish the task of religious education alone. The sooner church leaders and parents face this fact, the better it will be.[3]

Through the abilities of its individual members, the family makes a sizable contribution to church strength as it shares in the teaching and leadership responsibilities.

Through enthusiastic cooperation with and support of church educational efforts, the home provides both strength and encouragement to the church program. Parents helping children with Sunday school lessons, supporting youth regu-

---

[3]Findley B. Edge, *Teaching for Results* (Nashville: Broadman Press, 1956), p. 178.

lations, providing transportation and refreshments, and just being interested in activities are practical evidence of such support.

The very attitude of parents toward the church and Christian living, as well as their own practical example, provides a potent influence for the rest of the family.

Finally, the home supports the church program through regular giving, and by projects undertaken as a family, or in conjunction with other church families. Voluntary service often makes it possible to accomplish work which might otherwise not be done.

RELATIONSHIP OF HOME TO OTHER CHURCH AGENCIES

The home includes all age groups and touches each educational program. Church-home cooperation, therefore, should be evidenced in and through each organization, and the church will be wise to make every possible provision to draw the home into its planning and programming.

ORGANIZING FOR CHURCH-HOME COOPERATION

Personnel

In addition to the overall supervision of pastor, Christian education director, and board of Christian education, a parent-staff fellowship or a church-home committee can prove to be valuable. In some instances a separate sub-committee of the board of Christian education may serve in this way.

Program

The means by which the church and home work together may be grouped in three ways: the church going to the home, the home coming to the church, and the church and home going to the community.

THE CHURCH GOING TO THE HOME

Home visitation by church leadership is a vital part of establishing church-home rapport. W. Neill Hart suggests the following as purposes of home visits:

> Understanding the pupil being taught
> Establishing rapport between church and home
> Understanding the home and its needs
> Explaining work and securing cooperation
> Sharing pertinent literature
> Availability for counseling[4]

---

[4] W. Neill Hart, "What May Church and Home Do Together?" *Encyclopedia for Church Group Leaders*, ed. Lee J. Gable (New York: Association Press, 1959), pp. 303-305.

When regular visitation is not possible (and to supplement visitation), the church may periodically come to homes through a parents' bulletin or magazine. This not only provides information about church families, but can give helps for building Christian homes, guidance for family devotions, and Bible instruction. Also, appropriate church library books may be taken to homes and suggested as reading.

THE HOME COMING TO THE CHURCH

As families become involved in church activity other than the Sunday worship services, the opportunity to assist them is expanded. However, there must be a wise balance between church and home activity, and care must be exercised to keep the good from hindering the best.

Class instruction especially geared to home interests, such as family devotions and the Christian development of children, may serve well in helping to establish and strengthen Christian homes. Often adult elective Sunday school courses may be used to good effect. Weekday home study groups frequently provide both fellowship and learning. Social programs arranged at regular intervals may also encourage involvement by entire families and be the source of valuable learning experiences.

Periodic open house programs for parents and family groups by church organizations provide a lasting impression. Departmental parents' nights or visitation Sundays are helpful.

Parents who accept teaching or leadership positions within the church find this spiritual challenge carrying over into home matters. Others may assist by becoming department or class parents with responsibility for keeping in touch with pupils' parents and encouraging parental projects.

THE CHURCH AND HOME GOING TO THE COMMUNITY

Every family member cannot be a part of every church activity. However, it is important for every family member where possible to have a part in some church activity, and for church and families to work together in community outreach.

Community visitation programs, home Bible study classes under the sponsorship of the church, and cooperative programs relating to home problems offer a vital Christian contact with the community. Family suppers and social evenings to which community people can be invited and where they will meet Christian families are other means of outreach.

A church open house may provide an excellent opportunity for the community to learn what the church is attempting to do and which of their neighbors serve there.

Financing

Devotional material or a home magazine is sometimes provided for the home by the church or Sunday school. Beyond this, church-home cooperation financing is usually an integral part of the regular church budget.

SUMMARY

Church-home cooperation is an essential part of an effective Christian education program. Both the church and the home are strengthened by working closely together, and the individual believer gains much.

The church serves as a resource guide for parents, offering specialized information and counsel. The home reenforces the church's educational ministry both by its Christian witness and by its share in the educational leadership.

Besides the regular worship service and other weekly activities, the church ministers to the home through visitation, family paper or magazine, and purposeful social activities.

The church and home share in community outreach through visitation, home Bible study classes, social activities and open house programs.

Organization of church-home cooperation is often strengthened by a parent-staff fellowship or church-home committee related to the board of Christian education.

SHARING YOUR THINKING

1. Discuss early experiences that influenced your attitude toward Christianity and how effective church-home cooperation might have assured more positive results.
2. How might a young person's Christian development suffer were he to have no church, but depend wholly on the instruction of his family?
3. Discuss occasions when church and home responsibilities seem to be making conflicting demands and how this might be resolved.

PRACTICAL PROJECTS

1. List the major areas of Christian life and living in which a Christian young person should receive instruction. After each subject indicate the agency (church, home, school, or other) which should take the major responsibility, and how other agencies might cooperate.
2. Analyze a Christian periodical in terms of its help to each member of your family. For this purpose, you may wish to proceed by listing the names of the family members,

those articles pertinent to each, and the values of the information presented.
3. Outline a program for promoting Christian education in the family.

RESOURCES
Bibliography

Brandt, Henry, and Dowdy, Homer. **Building a Christian Home.** Wheaton, Ill.: Scripture Press, 1960.
> A readable volume, the text focuses Christianity on the individual, parents, and family circle.

DeJong, Alexander. **The Christian Family and Home.** Grand Rapids: Baker Book House, 1959.
> The material deals with practical matters, and provides thoughtful discussion questions.

Eavey, C. B. **Principles of Personality Building for Christian Parents.** Grand Rapids: Zondervan Publishing House, 1952.
> A helpful work, the title accurately describes its content.

Edge, Findley B. **Teaching for Results.** Nashville: Broadman Press, 1956.
> The text includes a chapter on home-church cooperation.

Erb, Alta Mae. **Christian Education in the Home.** Scottdale, Pa.: Herald Press, 1963.
> The emphasis in this brief work is placed on the child in the Christian home.

Inch, Morris A. "The Home as an Educational Agency," **An Introduction to Evangelical Christian Education** (J. Edward Hakes, ed.), Chicago: Moody Press, 1964.
> This survey chapter suggests a biblical ideal, along with historical development, and some observations of current practices.

Mow, Anna B. **Your Child.** Grand Rapids: Zondervan Publishing House, 1963.
> Experience orientated, the book seeks to relate the dynamics of human and divine life in children.

CHAPTER 3

The Sunday School

ANNA RIEGER

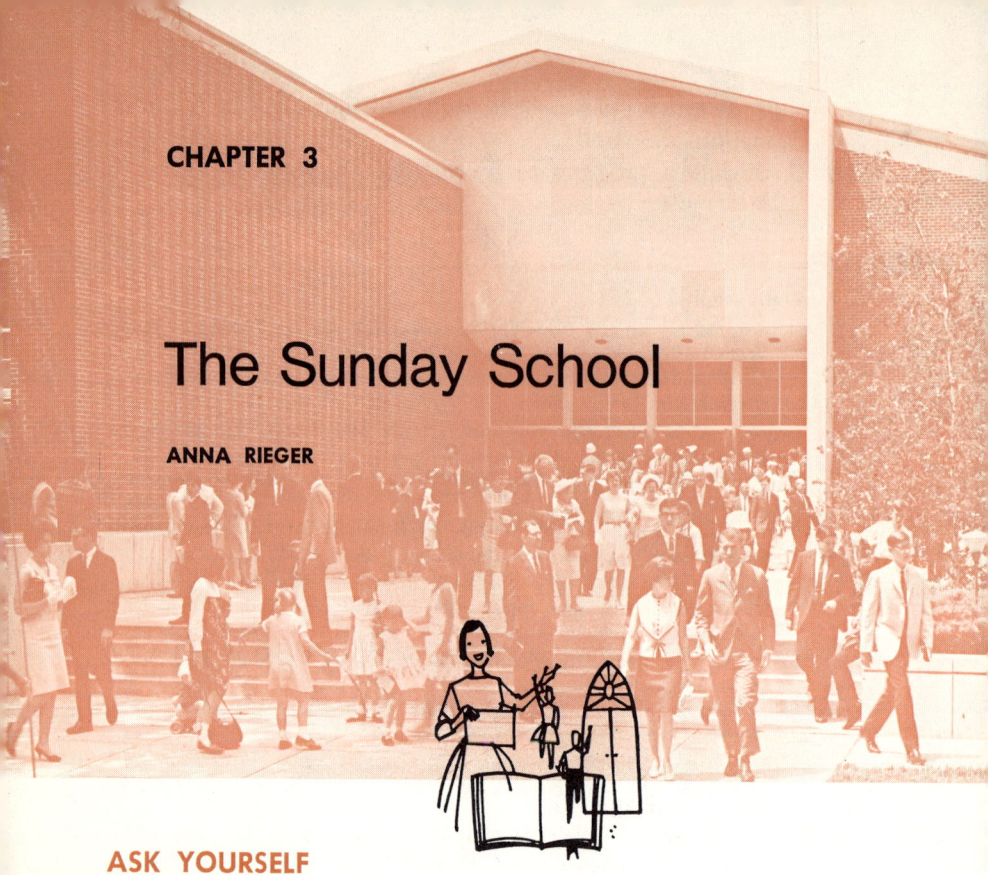

ASK YOURSELF

*These are questions to orient preclass thinking.
They may also be used as review after study.*

1. What is the distinctive purpose of the Sunday school in the church?
2. How did the Sunday school originate?
3. What is the biblical basis for the Sunday school?
4. What is meant by the statement that the teacher is the key to a successful Sunday school?
5. What training opportunities should be available to Sunday school workers?
6. What are some criteria that could guide a curriculum committee in selecting teaching materials for the Sunday school?

DO YOU KNOW?

The Sunday school is the leading agency in the organized teaching ministry of the church. It "exists to further the work of the church—to make disciples of all nations . . . it is the church functioning in a specific teaching ministry."[1] Both as a

---

[1]Mavis Anderson, *Charting the Course* (Harrisburg: Christian Publications, 1955), p. 12.

Anna Rieger, D.R.E., *formerly Grace Bible Institute faculty*

program for teaching people God's Word and as an effective evangelistic force, the Sunday school has been signally blessed by God for nearly two centuries.

What is the Sunday School?

The Sunday school is a church-sponsored educational agency which functions on Sunday and provides a curriculum of Bible study and evangelistic emphasis for all ages.

The Sunday school movement as such had its beginning in Gloucester, England, in the year 1780, although there were antecedents as far back as Old Testament times. Robert Raikes' purpose in beginning schools on Sunday was to teach children of the slum areas to read and write, and the Bible was used as a text.

The movement was received slowly and Raikes sometimes was severely criticized for "desecrating the Sabbath Day." However, among those who supported the effort were William Fox, founder of the first Sunday school society in England, and the brothers John and Charles Wesley. At the time of Raikes' death in 1811 there were thousands of Sunday schools in England and the movement was firmly established.

The Sunday school was started in America in 1785 and played an important role in shaping the national life of the country, especially in the frontier developments. As the Bible was gradually moved out of its original place in the public schools, the great task of teaching people God's Word was left largely to the Sunday school.

VALUES OF THE SUNDAY SCHOOL

There is great stress in both the Old and New Testaments on teaching. God commanded Moses to "gather the people together, men, and women, and children . . . that they may hear, and that they may learn, and . . . do all the words of this law" (Deut. 31:12). Parents are exhorted to bring up their children "in the nurture and admonition of the Lord" (Eph. 6:4). Christ, the Master Teacher, conducted a traveling school in which He taught a group of twelve disciples. The modern Sunday school carries on this teaching emphasis.

Provides for Systematic Teaching of the Bible

The Sunday school provides for systematic teaching of the Word of God and its application in Christian life and service. It offers opportunity for Bible study on a layman's level reaching all ages and all types of people at a regular time and place.

Presents Claims of Christ

The evangelical Sunday school presents the message of salvation to its pupils. Thus it has been at the forefront of evangelism in American history, and continues to offer the church one of its most potent soul-winning outreaches. It is pertinent to note that one of the Sunday school's most enthusiastic backers was the evangelist, Dwight L. Moody.

Gives Opportunity for Service

The Sunday school provides more opportunities for Christian service than any other agency in the church. There is need for teachers, secretaries, pianists, and a wide range of other interests and abilities. Even with limited formal training, the layman who is willing to prepare himself can find a place of useful service.

Promotes Church Growth

The Sunday school also is important because it promotes church growth and fruitfulness. It adds members to the body of Christ and to the church. It is a training ground for the preparation of leaders in other church endeavors. The Sunday school is indeed, as Clarence H. Benson has said, "the gold mine of the church."[2]

Builds Character

The Sunday school strengthens moral character. Mr. J. Edgar Hoover has frequently credited the Sunday school with being a major deterent to crime. The influence of the Sunday school on moral standards has been far-reaching and it continues to be a vital force in the building of Christian citizenship.

TYPES OF SUNDAY SCHOOL ORGANIZATION

Variations in Length

Most Sunday schools meet for one hour. However, by increasing this traditional length by fifteen minutes, the learning experience of every pupil is increased 25 percent. Some churches extend Sunday school sessions for children through church time. Such sessions can include class lessons, discussion, worship, and some play activity.

Variations in Time of Meeting

The problem of insufficient facilities for an active, growing Sunday school can sometimes be solved by time adjustments. Classes can be held before morning worship, between

---

[2]Clarence H. Benson, *The Sunday School in Action* (Chicago: Moody Press, 1941), p. 36.

two worship services, at the same times as two worship services are being held, or during the afternoon in a branch or extension Sunday school. Double session Sunday schools are operated either with complete duplicate classes, or with each session offering an assigned portion of the total classes.

Variations in Divisions

A simple division in the Sunday school is by school grade, and there is the further grouping of grades into departments. Departments may be composed of one, two, or three grades depending upon the size of the school.

The grading or departmentalization will be closely related to the choice of curriculum and planning for opening sessions.

RELATIONSHIP TO OTHER CHURCH AGENCIES

In the ever expanding educational outreach of the church, other agencies for Christian education have developed. Each of these being used in the local church should have a clearly defined purpose and position. While the Sunday school is usually the major teaching program of the church, such activities as boys' and girls' clubs and youth programs have an important ministry and must be carefully coordinated into the total program by such means as a board of Christian education.

ORGANIZATION IN THE SUNDAY SCHOOL

Organization in the Sunday school has to do with planning the curriculum and classes. Administration involves the procurement and supervision of the people who perform the work outlined in the planning. Efficient organization unifies a Sunday school and clarifies responsibility as it seeks to implement the objectives of the school.

Personnel

Because the success of the Sunday school depends so largely on the Christian personality and ability of the leadership, there is a vital need for loyal, energetic, large-visioned people who can assume the task with determination and devotion.

PASTOR

Unless a church is of sufficient size to engage a director of Christian education, the pastor carries a key responsibility for the program of Christian education. He should work closely with the Sunday school superintendent. The concerned pastor can inspire, energize, and counsel the Sunday school staff and lead in making the Sunday school a vital means of furthering the mission and ministry of the church.

SUPERINTENDENT

The supervision of the Sunday school requires educational vision, administrative ability, and untiring effort. The effective superintendent must believe in the Sunday school, be able to work with people, and have a genuine spiritual concern for those to whom the Sunday school ministers. He should be "more than a presiding officer at 'opening exercises' or a 'genial investigator' flitting about from place to place, dispensing smiling good will."[3]

OTHER OFFICERS

The department superintendent is responsible for the work in his department, guiding and encouraging the teachers. The school secretary can render important service to Christ and the Sunday school by recording minutes accurately, handling correspondence promptly, and supplying the church with meaningful statistics. The treasurer's task is one which requires honesty, accuracy, and promptness. Offering money should be taken care of properly. Other officers, such as departmental secretaries, music director, registrar, and librarian, are appointed as the needs arise.

TEACHERS

The teacher is the key to a successful Sunday school. It has been suggested that "ninety percent of the success of a Sunday school depends upon the teacher."[4] It is imperative, therefore, that the right persons be appointed to lead the Bible classes. Raffety once advised that a church should look for teachers who are personality-tested, pedagogically-minded, purposefully-motivated, and possessed of their senses, not the least of which is common sense."[5]

The successful Sunday school teacher will be in right personal relationship with God, learn all he can about the pupils he teaches, and study earnestly the Word of God and best methods of teaching. The teaching time in Sunday school is relatively short and the teacher must endeavor to use it to best advantage. He must allow the Holy Spirit to be his constant source of strength.

Program

While the Sunday school is specifically charged with the

---

[3] As expressed by Oliver DeWolf Cummings in *Christian Education in the Local Church*.
[4] D. K. Reisinger, Clate A. Risley (eds.), *Teach With Confidence* (Wheaton, Ill.: Evangelical Teacher Training Association and National Sunday School Association, 1965), p. 9.
[5] W. Edward Raffety, *How to Lead a Bible School* (Cincinnati: Standard Publishing, 1936), p. 38.

responsibility of teaching the Word of God, there should also be provision for such areas as teacher training, instruction in worship, and missionary education. Often these fit naturally into the regular curriculum of the school.

CURRICULUM MATERIALS

A Sunday school must exercise great care in selecting its course of study. The person or group responsible for choosing teaching materials should consider such questions as the following: Are the materials attractive? Are the theological emphases sound? Do the lessons encourage Bible study? Do they provide ample helps for the teacher?

EVANGELISM

An important task of the Sunday school is evangelism. The teacher should know each pupil's personal relationship to Christ and teach with the pupil's spiritual needs in mind. Training in Sunday school evangelism is an important part of the worker's preparation for Sunday school leadership.

LEADERSHIP AND SERVICE TRAINING

Because the Sunday school must draw its workers from the local church, leadership preparation becomes an essential part of any successful Sunday school effort. There is probably no more productive means for providing an adequate supply of leaders and insuring effective teaching than a long-range, high quality teacher training program.

Training can include formal teacher training classes, workers' conferences, and department workshops. Teachers may gain further help through a guided reading program, personal coaching, and attendance at Sunday school conventions.

Facilities and Equipment

Trained workers need adequate facilities and equipment to be fully effective. One writer has referred to the church building as the teacher's workshop and its equipment as his tools. Space needs usually relate to worship, teaching, expressional activities, and social activities. Minimum standards require that each classroom be clean and light, attractively decorated, and large enough for pupil comfort. The essential items of equipment include suitable chairs, tables of the right shape and height, space for hanging wraps, and supply cupboards. Chalkboards and tack boards are also on the list of essentials, as well as tuned pianos, play equipment for younger children, and conveniently located toilet facilities.

Financing

The Sunday school is included in the church budget, and

as church members give according to God's plan there should be ample funds to carry on a good program of Christian education through the Sunday school.[6]

SUMMARY

From its origin in England in 1780, the Sunday school has developed into the church's leading educational agency. It provides opportunity for systematic Bible study for all ages, as well as being a vital means for evangelistic outreach.

Because it is essentially a lay movement, the work depends largely upon local church leadership preparation to provide workers and to insure effective teaching. The Sunday school offers the largest opportunity of any church agency for church members to use their abilities and service for Christ.

SHARING YOUR THINKING

1. Discuss the dividing of pupils into groups according to public school grades as over against grouping according to age.
2. Discuss the place of evangelism as it relates to each division of the Sunday school.
3. Discuss a major need of your Sunday school and what can be done about it in the next six months.

PRACTICAL PROJECTS

1. Prepare a detailed job analysis for the general superintendent in a Sunday school of two hundred pupils.
2. Make a chart of all the classes of your Sunday school, indicating how you would handle a fifty percent increase in attendance.
3. Make a comparative study of a drab, unsatisfactory Sunday school room for preschool pupils and a satisfactory one, showing how the first room can be changed into the second at minimum cost.

RESOURCES

Bibliography

Benson, Clarence H. **The Sunday School in Action.** Chicago: Moody Press, 1941.
    The author deals with the organization and administration of the Sunday school.

_____. **Sunday School Success.** Wheaton, Ill.: Evangelical Teacher Training Association, 1964.
    This is a unit of the Certificate Series of materials for use in

---

[6]R. O. Woodworth, *How to Operate a Sunday School* (Grand Rapids: Zondervan Publishing House, 1961), chapter 19.

teacher training classes and contains twelve lessons on Sunday school administration.

Byrne, H. W. **Christian Education for the Local Church.** Grand Rapids: Zondervan Pub. House, 1963.

    Chapters 5, 6, and 7 contain helpful information which delineates the qualifications and responsibilities of the general superintendent, department superintendent, and teachers in the Sunday school.

Hakes, J. Edward (ed.). **An Introduction to Evangelical Christian Education.** Chicago: Moody Press, 1964.

    This book covers many areas of Sunday school work. Chapter 23 is on Sunday school history and trends.

Leavitt, Guy P. **Teach With Success.** Cincinnati: Standard Publishing, 1956.

    A concentrated manual on the preparation of the Christian teacher, methods of teaching the Bible lesson, and evaluating teaching.

LeBar, Lois. **Children in the Bible School.** Westwood, N. J.: Fleming H. Revell Co., 1952.

    Discusses child development, the teaching setting, and methods of teaching children in the Sunday school and church.

Richards, Lawrence O. (ed.). **The Key to Sunday School Achievement.** Chicago: Moody Press, 1965.

    A "measuring stick" designed to evaluate Sunday schools and to use as a step-by-step guide to greater Sunday school effectiveness.

Sunday School Encyclopedia, Volumes XI, XII. Chicago: National Sunday School Association, 1962, 1965.

    A compilation of articles on many phases of the Sunday school and Christian education by specialists in the field. The articles are summary outlines of workshops given at national Sunday school conventions.

Woodworth, R. O. **How to Operate a Sunday School.** Grand Rapids: Zondervan Publishing House, 1961.

    A manual prepared primarily for Sunday school superintendents, outlining the basic responsibilities involved in directing the work of a school.

Related National Service Agencies

EVANGELICAL TEACHER TRAINING ASSOCIATION
Box 327, Wheaton, Ill. 60187

CHAPTER 4

Weekday Bible Classes

RUTH C. HAYCOCK

ASK YOURSELF

These are questions to orient preclass thinking. They may also be used as review after study.

1. What types of weekday classes are being used in Christian education?
2. How does a church benefit from weekday Bible classes?
3. What factors enter into the decision as to the type of weekday program to be initiated?
4. What steps should be taken in beginning a weekday program?
5. How does a church administer a weekday teaching program?

DO YOU KNOW?

The early New Testament church used weekday classes, meeting in homes and in the temple, to propagate the Gospel and develop believers (Acts 2:46; 5:42). This method undoubtedly had an important place in the rapid spread of Christianity and in the vitality of the first century believers.

Church interest in weekday teaching has been reviving and there is a renewed emphasis on home Bible classes, weekday church schools, and similar programs.

Ruth C. Haycock, Ed.D., *Baptist Bible College of Pa. faculty*

What Are Weekday Bible Classes (Church-Sponsored)?

They are church-related Bible instruction programs which meet on weekdays, and include classes during school hours where pupils are released from public school for religious instruction; neighborhood classes meeting in homes at daytime or evening hours; and evening institutes, where adults are offered a variety of courses.

VALUES OF THE PROGRAM

Additional Time for Teaching the Bible

What Sunday school teacher has not at some time complained of the shortness of time for teaching the Bible? Almost every church is aware of its limitations in providing adequate instruction. Weekday teaching periods, therefore, offer a practical addition to the church's teaching ministry.

Witness Beyond Church Family

Weekday classes reach out into the community with Bible teaching. Many adults who will not attend regular church services have an opportunity to hear the Word taught and are reached with the Gospel message. Often a large percentage of the children enrolled in weekday classes are not attending Sunday school.

Encouragement to Witness

Meeting people where they are and showing them the application of the Scriptures to their everyday lives is a special ministry of weekday groups. Teachers and pupils meet in more relaxed, informal situations than normally are possible in the Sunday program.

TYPES OF STUDY PROGRAMS

Programs for Children

WEEKDAY CHURCH SCHOOL OR RELEASED TIME CLASSES

In some states[*] children may be released from public school during school hours to attend religious instruction classes in the church chosen by their parents. Such permission is a recognition on the part of school authorities of the importance of religion. Whether these classes are geared primar-

[*]According to information gathered in 1963 by a national church organization, states which specifically *permit* dismissal for religious instruction are the following: Calif., Ind., Ky., Mass., Mich., Minn., Nev., N.J., N.Y., Ohio, Ore., Pa., and Va.; states which have declared released time classes *illegal* are Colo., Del., and Wis.; other states apparently have no ruling. For information about the current status in a particular state, write to the Department of Education at the state capitol.

ily to the youth of the sponsoring church or to a wider group depends on what other religious instruction classes are conducted in the community.

HOME BIBLE CLASSES

Home classes are less formal than the released time classes and cover a wider age span. A hostess invites neighborhood school children to a weekly after school Bible club, taught by a teacher from her church. Preschool clubs usually meet in homes following naptime.

Programs for Youth and Adults

HOME BIBLE CLASSES

Some churches encourage interested couples to invite neighbors in for a weekly evening of Bible study. In other cases there may be daytime studies for women, for retired persons, or for institutionalized groups.

EVENING INSTITUTES

Larger churches may establish evening institutes for courses in addition to those taught on Sunday. Most institutes offer several courses in one evening. Where one church is unable to open an evening institute alone, several churches band together to have the benefit of a variety of courses and instructors. Cooperative schools also benefit by broader promotional outreach and student recruitment.

RELATIONSHIP TO THE CHURCH

To be church-related means that groups are established by the church, their leadership approved, their curriculums correlated with the total church educational program, and the church's responsibility clearly delineated.

Group Established

The decision to begin any new program should be based on a consideration of the goals of the church, what the program offers, what it involves, and how it relates to what is already being done. Careful study must be given to determine whether it is best to begin a new agency, or to strengthen existing programs.

Leadership Approved

Weekday workers and teachers are normally appointed in the same manner as Sunday school workers, preferably by a board of Christian education. While it is right that each agency seek the best possible leaders, it is also vital that each worker be helped to find the place where he can contribute most.

Curriculums Correlated

All agencies of the church, including weekday programs, should strengthen the total church ministry. To assure this, it is essential to study carefully the aims, program, curriculum, materials, and methods of each weekday activity and work toward correlation in each area.

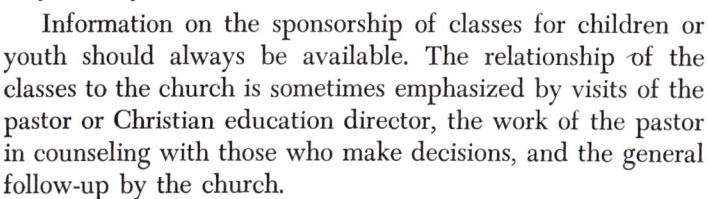

Responsibility Delineated

Information on the sponsorship of classes for children or youth should always be available. The relationship of the classes to the church is sometimes emphasized by visits of the pastor or Christian education director, the work of the pastor in counseling with those who make decisions, and the general follow-up by the church.

In all weekday activities those who come to personal faith in Christ should be encouraged in Christian witness and growth through fellowship with a local church.

ORGANIZING WEEKDAY CLASSES

Included in organizing are these preliminary steps: set up the schedule; arrange housing; recruit the staff; recommend and obtain teaching materials; and plan details of inviting prospects and securing parental permissions.

It is also important to provide orientation and training for workers; determine suitable methods of record-keeping and follow-up; promote and publicize the program; and plan regular reports to the church or churches involved.

Personnel

An organized weekday activity often requires the appointment of a director, who works with the pastor and the board of Christian education. In the case of released time programs, it is especially important to have qualified teachers who will maintain a favorable comparison to the teaching quality of the schools.

FOR WEEKDAY CHURCH SCHOOL

The availability of qualified teachers is a factor in determining which type of Bible teaching program should be initiated for children. Since public schools often prefer to release all pupils at one time, a weekday church school may require many teachers.

Classes must be small enough for effective teaching. Disorder is both a poor testimony and a loss of teaching opportunity. One teacher and assistant should be able to teach fifteen children; expert teachers may be able to handle larger groups. Where children are released at staggered hours churches may desire to employ trained full-time workers.

Generally, the pastor or director of Christian education makes the initial contact with cooperating churches and the public school authorities for a released time program.

FOR HOME BIBLE CLASSES

In a home Bible class program the director or person responsible locates homes and secures teachers and lesson material, under the guidance of the Christian education board. It may also be necessary to have teacher training classes before beginning the program, or provide review sessions concurrently with the Bible classes.

Although a home program for adults does not require the same supervision as children's classes, every effort should be made to maintain orderly procedures and provide for the conserving of teaching results.

FOR EVENING INSTITUTES

When an evening institute involves several churches, pastors or their representatives normally select an institute director and committee, who then do most of the organizational work. It is well to use workers from each of the cooperating churches, since interest within each church is encouraged by participation in planning and operation. In a one-church institute the director and committee are selected by the appropriate church board.

Institutes are staffed by pastors and other persons who have had specialized training for the subjects to be taught.

Program

WEEKDAY CHURCH SCHOOL

Where many children are enrolled in a weekday school, grading should follow the public school pattern. Homogenous classes enable a teacher to gear presentation, activities, and application to a specific level. Where the situation does not permit close grading, classes may include two or three grades, as in a small Sunday school, with lesson series rotated from year to year.

Whether an opening assembly should supplement the class period depends on space, time, and age span. When the period is short, movement of groups wastes time.

Where children are untaught in the Bible, teaching content must be basic and teaching emphasis evangelistic. If most children are from the church, lessons must be distinct from those already in use in the church program. Often there is a mixture of new and old pupils and the teacher must strive to meet individual needs as much as possible.

HOME BIBLE CLASSES

Each children's session includes a Bible lesson with discussion, Scripture memorization, and music related to the teaching. In reaching youngsters of varied ages, the use of well chosen audiovisual materials is a great asset.

Home classes for adults often use Bible correspondence courses, individual books of the Bible, or topical studies, with or without study manuals.

EVENING INSTITUTES

Evening institute programs usually have a regular program of courses. These offer training in Bible, doctrine, Christian education, and related subjects for advanced workers as well as beginners. Regular pupil preparation is required and certificates are awarded for completion of work.

Often an established program of studies, such as the Evangelical Teacher Training Association Preliminary and Advanced series, is used. The Association has available both textbooks and teacher guides.

Facilities, Equipment, and Finance

Facilities and equipment adequate for an effective Sunday program are generally also satisfactory for a weekday church school or an evening institute. Though a weekday church school should aim to provide for all grades, limitation of space may recommend restriction to a few selected grades or the substitution of home classes.

Church sponsorship includes responsibility for furnishing teaching texts, an adequate record system, and the visual aids needed in the lesson presentation.

The financing of weekday programs is normally through the regular church budget. Such income is sometimes augmented by designated contributions, special offerings, or registration fees.

SUMMARY

Weekday Bible classes, with roots going back to New Testament times, are having an increased place of ministry in church educational programs. Major forms of activity are released time classes, neighborhood Bible classes, and evening institutes for Bible and related study.

Although important for each activity, qualified teachers are especially vital for effective released time classes. For these classes, and also evening institutes, a director is usually appointed to administer the program.

Significant values of weekday activities include the increase of church teaching time and enlarged neighborhood Gospel outreach.

SHARING YOUR THINKING

1. What specific steps would you take to begin a weekday church school?
2. Discuss in detail what is already being done in your community in weekday religious instruction.
3. What are the advantages and problems in a cooperative weekday school as compared with a one-church school?
4. Discuss the value of church sponsorship of home Bible classes.

PRACTICAL PROJECTS

1. Visit a weekday church school and prepare a report on attendance-taking and other routines, sizes of classes, materials used, and teaching methods.
2. Interview a teacher or hostess in an active home Bible class to discover who is reached, the types of decisions made, and the materials used.
3. Visit an evening institute. Obtain copies of its schedule, interview the director or dean, and discuss the practicality of such a school for your church or group of churches.

RESOURCES

Bibliography

Note: Although not all references specifically concern church sponsored classes, the material is adaptable for this type of program.

Periodicals

Bible Club Reporter. Monthly publication of the Bible Club Movement.
Evangelizing Today's Child. Bi-monthly publication of Child Evangelism Fellowship.

Sources of Curriculum Materials

Suggestions included here are limited to material for home Bible classes and weekday church schools, since evening institute instruction is very broad. Because there is a scarcity of graded Bible-centered materials designed for weekday church school, many churches adapt courses prepared for other purposes.

For Children's Classes

Barnhouse, Donald G., **Teaching the Word of Truth.** Grand Rapids: Wm. B. Eerdmans Publishing Co., 1958.
  Eighty doctrinal lessons illustrated by simple chalk drawings.
Bible Club Movement. **Footsteps of Faith.**
  A four-year Bible course with flannelboard figures. Several short-

er series also available, including **Tiny Steps of Faith** for preschoolers.

Child Evangelism Fellowship.
>Many one and two semester courses, with visual materials. Both topical and chronological series. Write for catalog.

For Youth and Adults

Bible Club Movement. **Steps to Maturity.**
>An in-depth Bible study course for teens and adults.

Christian Outreach.
>Topical workbook studies; also **Growth by Groups**, a year's program for serious believers. Church sponsorship required.

Inter-Varsity Press.
>Excellent discussion Bible studies designed for college students.

Moody Bible Institute Correspondence School.
>Many courses, including Bible surveys, Bible book studies, topical studies.

Neighborhood Bible Studies.
>Series of 16 guides for adult discussion study using the inductive study approach. Write for catalog.

Roper Press.
>"Through the Bible Study" workbooks in 6 series for youth and adults. Twelve units cover the whole Bible in 6 years, 26 lessons per unit. Usable individually or in groups. Material undated.

Walker, Catherine B. **Bible Workbook.** Chicago: Moody Press; Vol. I, 1951; Vol. 2, 1951.
>Each volume covers one Testament, with daily lessons for one semester for high school students. Adaptable to weekly classes.

Publishers' Addresses

BIBLE CLUB MOVEMENT, INC.
>237 Fairfield Avenue, Upper Darby, Pa. 19082

CHILD EVANGELISM FELLOWSHIP
>P.O. Box 1156, Grand Rapids, Mich. 49501

CHRISTIAN OUTREACH
>Box 22037, Ft. Lauderdale, Fla. 33315

EERDMANS, WM. B., PUBLISHING CO.
>255 Jefferson Ave., S.E., Grand Rapids, Mich. 49502

INTER-VARSITY PRESS
>Box F, Downers Grove, Ill. 60515

MOODY BIBLE INSTITUTE CORRESPONDENCE SCHOOL
>820 N. LaSalle St., Chicago, Ill. 60610

MOODY PRESS
>820 N. LaSalle St., Chicago, Ill. 60610

NEIGHBORHOOD BIBLE STUDIES
>Box 222, Dobbs Ferry, N.Y. 10522

ROPER PRESS
>6441 Gaston Ave., Dallas, Texas 75214

CHAPTER 5

Vacation Bible School

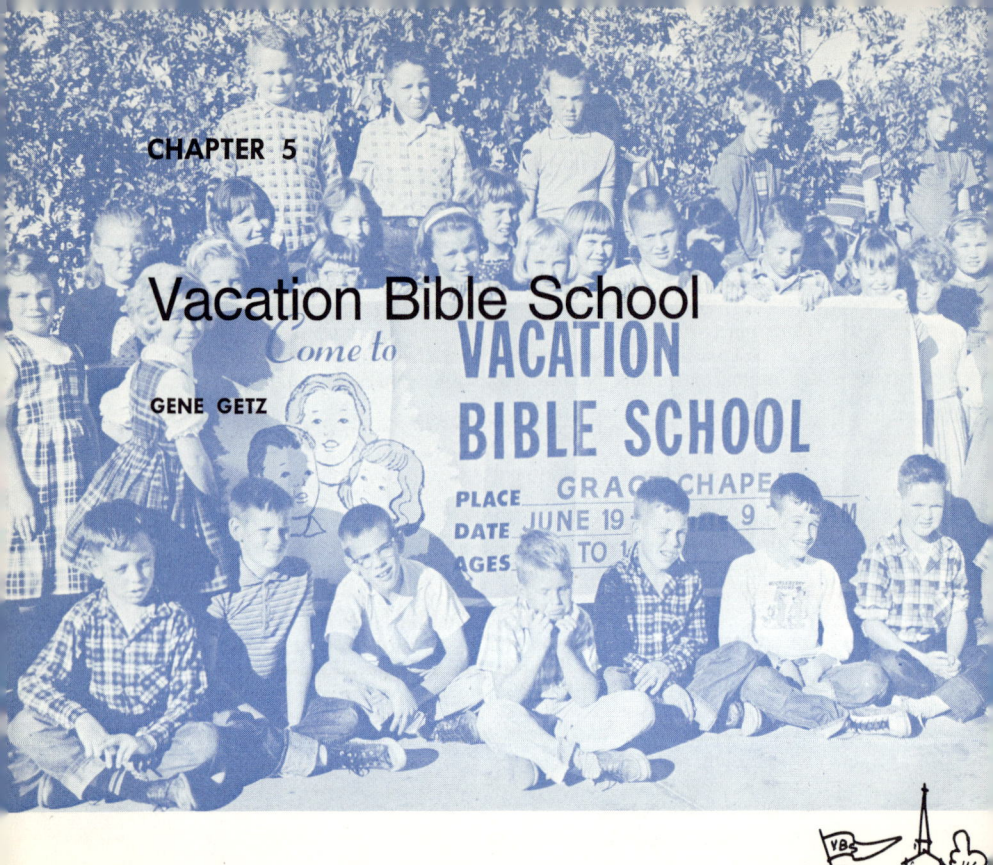

GENE GETZ

ASK YOURSELF

These are questions to orient preclass thinking.
They may also be used as review after study.

1. What is a vacation Bible school?
2. What are the values of a VBS to a church and its people?
3. How does VBS relate to the total church program?
4. What are the basic steps in preliminary planning necessary for a VBS?
5. What emphases are given in a balanced VBS program?
6. How can VBS results be conserved for the church?

DO YOU KNOW?

A well-conducted ten-day vacation Bible school can provide as much Christian education opportunity as a full half year of Sunday school. The current interest in adult education is increasingly opening up the VBS to all age groups. Also, considerable experimentation is being done with the use of VBS program during Easter vacation, in day camps, and through other channels. Vacation Bible school is indeed an important educational ministry of the local church.

Gene Getz, Ph.D., *Dallas Theological Seminary*

What is Vacation Bible School?

Vacation Bible school is a weekday school of Christian education for all ages, conducted by the church during a vacation period, with a program of Bible study and related activities.

It is still called a *vacation* Bible school because it is conducted primarily during vacation periods.

It is called a vacation *Bible* school because its basic purpose is to teach the Word of God.

It is called a vacation Bible *school* in that students meet together for a definite period of study under guidance of prepared teachers using a set curriculum.

VALUES OF VACATION BIBLE SCHOOL

Since its beginning at the turn of the century, VBS has made a large contribution to the ministry of Christian education.

Evangelistic Opportunity

Bible-centered study day after day enables a teacher to build a consistent evangelistic emphasis. Likewise, student-teacher rapport built by daily contacts provides opportunity for conversation leading to conversion. The result often is a rich spiritual harvest.

Sunday School and Church Growth

Because VBS reaches out into the community in a unique way, and at a receptive time, it often attracts new members to the Sunday school and makes contacts for future church growth.

Aid to Homes in Christian Training

A well organized VBS will involve whole families in the program either as students or teachers. This communication of the Gospel to family groups during a comparatively relaxed time of the year often makes opportunity for a far-reaching impact in spiritual matters.

Recruitment of Local Church Leaders

VBS has served as a vital agency in helping to discover and train new workers for other agencies in the church. Inexperienced workers volunteer help which if guided can prove to be an asset for the total church educational program. Older young people gain experience in leadership which can often be transferred to other church activities.

A Balanced Educational Program

Agencies in the church often have one particular educational emphasis. A major value of VBS is that it offers a balanced program of varied emphases. There is *instruction* in the Word of God and related areas such as missions and music. There is a *worship* program each day, along with *fellowship* opportunities, particularly during the recreational period. Finally, there are many opportunities for *service* within the VBS itself as pupils become involved in projects.

TYPES OF VACATION BIBLE SCHOOL

It is important in planning for a VBS to determine the type of school to be conducted. Schools vary according to who sponsors the school, when it is held, and for whom it is intended.

According to Sponsorship

In most instances, VBS is an *individual church school,* that is, it is conducted by one local church.

Some have found a *cooperative school* involving more than one church to be an effective type of ministry in certain communities. Community impact is often expanded and the efficient use of facilities and staff is made possible.

In addition to their own VBS, some churches conduct *branch schools* or *itinerant schools.* The itinerant school is a school where a team of workers will travel from place to place in a rural or thinly populated section of the country and conduct a number of small schools over a period of several weeks. Opportunity for ministry is given to many and the witness of the sponsoring church shared with an enlarged community.

According to Time

Three factors are involved in determining the time of vacation Bible schools. These factors are the length of time the school will continue, the hours of the day during which the school will be held, and the time of the year in which the VBS will be conducted.

LENGTH OF TIME

The standard length of a VBS has been two weeks or ten days. However, because of full programs of other summer Christian education activities, as well as community factors, some churches have effectively conducted one-week schools. Where possible, it is advisable, of course, to conduct a ten-day school to take fullest advantage of the concentrated educational and evangelistic opportunities of VBS.

TIME OF DAY

VBS may be conducted during the morning, afternoon, or early evening hours. Some churches have a combination program with a morning school for children up through the age of eleven and an evening school for youth and adults.

TIME OF YEAR

Most churches prefer to conduct vacation Bible school immediately upon the close of the public school. However, some have found that a July or August school can also be very effective. A helpful principle is that the school should be planned for the time when the majority of the potential pupils and workers are free from local work and vacation trips.

According to Age

CHILDREN ONLY

This enables a centering of interest upon those most willing to come, and cements relationships with families by serving their children.

CHILDREN AND YOUTH

When youth are included in VBS, two approaches are frequently used. One is to incorporate the young people into service as assistants, training them for teaching, and giving them Bible study.

The second pattern is to conduct a children's VBS in the morning and a youth Bible institute each evening. In this way the young people can serve in the morning and have their own evening activities.

ALL AGES

When all ages are in VBS it is frequently held in the evening to enable special studies for adults and youth and to provide for a total family VBS fellowship.

RELATIONSHIP OF VACATION BIBLE SCHOOL TO THE TOTAL CHURCH EDUCATIONAL PROGRAM

Other Organizations

Because VBS meets for such a brief time each year, it must be carefully related to continuing church activities if results are to be conserved.

Educational Leaders

The pastor should support his VBS from the pulpit and encourage the workers along the way. In a small church he may be the only person possessing the training and the ability to effectively guide the VBS program.

Where there is a director of Christian education, he works

closely with the VBS superintendent, giving guidance, instruction, and encouragement where needed.

Board of Christian Education

VBS is included in the responsibility of the board of Christian education. Usually, the board initiates the program by establishing a VBS planning committee.

Planning Committee

This committee has both direct and indirect responsibilities. Direct responsibilities include such matters as: evaluation of previous VBS; type of VBS to be held; time for the VBS; a VBS calendar (schedule of steps to be taken prior to VBS); selection of the workers; recommendation of the curriculum; an adequate financial program.

Indirect responsibilities are those that may be carried out by the planning committee or may be delegated to an individual or to another committee. These include: leadership training; adequate housing; transportation; promotion; conducting preregistration; worker dedication service; demonstration program; proper follow-up and conservation of results.

VBS Calendar

Early in the year it is important for the VBS planning committee to set up a tentative calendar. Dates should include such items as the VBS committee meetings, general staff meetings, leadership training sessions, individual department meetings, special preregistration periods, and, of course, the dates of the school. This calendar should be submitted to the board of Christian education so that it can be integrated into the total church calendar.

ORGANIZING A VACATION BIBLE SCHOOL

Personnel

RECRUITING AND APPOINTING WORKERS

Dedicated Christian leaders are a vital necessity for a VBS. Positions include: the general superintendent or director, department superintendents, teachers, the general secretary and treasurer, department secretaries, general helpers, pianists, and a craft leader.

If possible, all VBS workers should be approved by the board of Christian education. In some churches the board of Christian education, or the VBS committee, selects departmental leadership for the school. These leaders, in turn, select qualified workers for their departments. If the church has a Christian education personnel committee the responsibility for selecting all VBS workers could be theirs.

TRAINING WORKERS

The ideal plan for leadership training is to have a perennial training program where materials such as the E.T.T.A. courses are used. There may also be special VBS leadership training sessions and workshops, regular staff meetings, and departmental sessions. All workers should be encouraged to engage in individual study in order to prepare themselves for their particular part in the program.

DEDICATING WORKERS

Prior to the opening of the VBS, a dedication service for the workers should be planned. Ideally, this should become a part of the morning worship service.

Program

GROUPING

The normal plan for VBS grouping is to have all of the regular departments that are found in the Sunday school program.

ESTABLISHING CURRICULUM

VBS curriculum materials should be chosen on the basis of evangelical witness, denominational recommendation, and the adaptability of the materials to local needs. Excellent courses are available, and the majority are organized on a departmentally graded basis.[1]

Most materials include a record system, and carefully kept records assist greatly in planning and assuring lasting results.

DAILY PROGRAM

Daily programs are carefully worked out in the published curriculum materials. Programs for children usually include: presession activities, platform activities, class and recreational activities, post session activities.

Presession activities are those which take place prior to the opening time of the school. They often include a staff prayer meeting as well as student projects.

Platform activities are conducted for the entire departmental group and include flag salutes and worship activities. It is also practical to have one of the best story tellers present the Bible story to the total departmental group each day.

Class activities are those which will be carried on in a small group. They include discussion of the Bible story and its application, the use of the pupil's manual, and the craft time. Recreation, when the weather permits, is usually conducted on the playground or church lawn.

---

[1] See Resource section for a list of publishers.

DEMONSTRATION PROGRAM

The time to begin planning the demonstration program is before VBS begins. However, preparation for the program on the final evening usually continues throughout the VBS schedule.

CONSERVING RESULTS

Following VBS, emphasis should be given to conserving results. This may be aided through a closing VBS picnic and other follow-up activities. In an evaluation session, needs and problems can be recorded in order to make the program better the following year. In conserving spiritual results, nothing can replace a personal contact with the pupil through special letters or visits by the teachers, other leaders in the VBS program, or the pastor.

Facilities

Where church educational facilities are inadequate, school facilities may often be rented. Some have used tents and other temporary housing on the church property to provide added space.

Financing

Normally VBS expenses are included in the church Christian education budget. Special offerings received prior to the school and on demonstration night sometimes supplement the budget.

When offerings are received from the pupils, they can aid in teaching stewardship by being used for missionary projects at home or abroad.

SUMMARY

The vacation Bible school offers the church an opportunity for concentrated Bible teaching during an especially receptive time of the year. It also commends itself as a balanced program of Christian education that is able to include instruction, worship, fellowship, and service in its schedule.

Because of its relatively brief period of activity, its values and successes are closely related to how well it is integrated into the total, ongoing church program.

An essential in VBS planning is the VBS calendar. Included in the calendar should be all of the specific details and events that are related to the local VBS program.

SHARING YOUR THINKING

1. Why is evaluation an especially important factor in a VBS program?

2. What circumstances in a community would justify conducting a cooperative VBS?
3. What important factors should be considered in selecting VBS curriculum materials?

PRACTICAL PROJECTS

1. Secure several sets of sample VBS materials from different publishers and evaluate them as a group. Look for strengths and weaknesses.
2. Work out a VBS planning calendar for your church, with the calendar beginning right after the closing program.
3. Plan and write out a dedication service for VBS workers.

RESOURCES

Bibliography

Burnett, Sibley C. **Better Vacation Bible Schools.** Nashville: Convention Press, 1957.
   One of the books in the Southern Baptist training series.

Clark, Ruth A. **Vacation Bible School.** Wheaton, Ill.: Evangelical Teacher Training Association, 1959, rev. 1964.
   Evangelical Teacher Training textbook with twelve practical chapters.

Getz, Gene A. **The Vacation Bible School in the Local Church.** Chicago: Moody Press, 1962.
   A textbook of fifteen chapters prepared for use in the college classroom or in the church.

Latham, Mary E. **Vacation Bible Schools Why, What and How?** Kansas City: Beacon Hill Press, 1954.
   A VBS planning guide going from need to follow-up.

Publishers of Materials

ALDERSGATE
   2923 Troost Ave., Box 527, Kansas City, Mo. 64109
CONCORDIA PUBLISHING HOUSE
   3558 S. Jefferson Ave., St. Louis, Mo. 63118
GOSPEL LIGHT PUBLICATIONS
   P.O. Box 1591, Glendale, Calif. 91209
HERALD PRESS
   610 Walnut Ave., Scottdale, Pa. 15683
SCRIPTURE PRESS PUBLICATIONS
   1825 College Ave., Wheaton, Ill. 60187
STANDARD PUBLISHING
   8121 Hamilton Ave., Cincinnati, Ohio 45231

CHAPTER 6

Church Camping

PAUL R. FINK

ASK YOURSELF

These are questions to orient preclass thinking. They may also be used as review after study.

1. What do we mean by "church camping"?
2. What are the different types of camping?
3. What are the distinctive values of church camping as an educational ministry?
4. What should be included in a daily camp schedule?
5. What qualifications should a camp counselor have?
6. What organization is needed to carry on a church camping program?

DO YOU KNOW?

Church camping is a growing part of the church's Christian education ministry.

Christian camping is here to stay . . . It is safe to say that at the present time there is hardly a church organization large enough to support a camp which is not in the process of renting, site-seeking or improving the camp which it now possesses.[1]

---

[1]*Guiding Principles for Christian Camping* (Wheaton, Ill.: National Sunday School Association, 1962), p. 1.

Paul R. Fink, Th.D., *Grace Theological Seminary faculty*

Camping, in the simple definition of outdoor living, has been a part of man's history from earliest records, and for many it has been a normal way of life. In the Bible there are many references that fit into this category. It is recorded that Abraham, for example, "pitched his tent" (Gen. 12:8), and the Israelites in their wanderings were told to "pitch their tents, every man by his own camp" (Num. 1:52).

However, modern organized camping is a development of the past hundred years, and church camping is closely related to the Christian education movement of the past half century.

What Is Church Camping?

Church camping is a church-sponsored program of group living in an outdoor setting, seeking to fulfill appropriate Christian education objectives.

A growing development in the Christian camping field is the Christian day camp, which is opening up new opportunities for summer teaching ministry. It has the advantage of offering a camp-type experience without the necessity of extensive camp facilities. Trip camping is also being used as a church ministry in many areas.

VALUES OF CHURCH CAMPING

Church camping offers unique opportunities in Christian education. Gilbert emphasizes this in his discussion on the setting for learning as he notes that "church camps have certain characteristics which give them tremendous educational potential."[2]

A good summary of some educational values is given by Hammett and Musselman in their book on camp program. The values they list include: the setting is different; the activities are different; the group experience is different; there is more time; there is isolation; there is close leader-group relationship; there is readiness on the part of the campers.[3]

Each of these values has application to church camping. The *different setting* of camping, for instance, provides a fresh natural environment in which young people can prayerfully consider and reevaluate their Christian life. Away from the pressures of peer groups and the hurried pace of present-day living, youth can make new decisions and dedications.

---

[2]W. Kent Gilbert, *As Christians Teach* (Philadelphia: Lutheran Church Press, 1962), p. 92.
[3]Catherine T. Hammett and Virginia Musselman, *The Camp Program Book* (New York: Association Press, 1951), pp. 4-7.

The time factor, as camping provides for 24-*hour a day experience,* is an outstanding teaching potential for practical Christian living. As individuals live together day after day in normal activities, Christianity becomes related to all of life.

The *close leader-group relationship* is also a major value for Christian camping. The witness of dedicated Christian camp counselors is undoubtedly one of the major influences of the church camp. Here again, the normal daily living of the camp provides natural opportunities for counseling that rarely occur in other church activities.

These values are consistently attested to by those who have shared in the Christian camp experience. Decision for Christ and Christian growth result from a well-organized program of Christian camping.

TYPES OF CAMPING PROGRAMS

There are various ways of classifying camps. Perhaps the first distinction should be made between the camp and the conference (or "conference type camp," as termed by the Camp Commission of the N.S.S.A.). While there are points of similarity and overlapping program factors, the conference is usually identified as being platform centered, employing more mass activity, and using natural environment as a secondary program factor.

The camp, on the other hand, tends to emphasize small-group activity, importance of the cabin counselor, and use of the outdoor setting. The place of a camp speaker may vary in such a program. The Todds have a listing of other distinguishing features.[4]

Camps themselves can be classified by age groups (including family camping), and by special interests such as music, sports, and similar categories.

However, the most basic classification of camps is normally in terms of the following:

Resident Camp

The resident camp is conducted on a permanent site. Campers live on this site for a period of time, usually one to two weeks, although this may also vary from the short winter weekend camp to a long-term summer camp of several months. Normally there are permanent camp facilities, and the camp may be owned or used on some type rental arrangement by the church group.

---

[4] Floyd and Pauline Todd, *Camping for Christian Youth* (New York: Harper & Row, 1963), p. 30.

Day Camp

As the name implies, the day camp is held only during the day. The campers sleep at home and usually eat only one meal at the camp. The camp facilities vary from very elaborate camp sites to church recreation areas. The day's program may include a wide variety of camping activities.

Trail Camp

The trail camp has no permanent facilities, although it may be part of a resident camp program. Its basic characteristic is its mobility, and it is sometimes therefore referred to as "trip camp." Mode of travel includes backpack, canoe, or horseback.

RELATIONSHIP TO OTHER CHURCH EDUCATIONAL AGENCIES

Church camping is an educational agency of the church. As such, it is administered by the board of Christian education. It is important that the other church agencies understand the ministry of camping as supplementing and strengthening the total Christian program. As in the case of vacation Bible school, the seasonal aspect of camping requires that there be close relationship and follow-up through the other educational agencies to conserve results.

ORGANIZING CHURCH CAMPING

Organizing a camping program can involve specialized areas which are beyond the scope of this chapter to cover. Two such areas are camp site development and camp management.

The purchasing and developing of a camp site is a subject that requires considerable separate study. Some of the books listed in the Bibliography, such as the one by the Todds, have chapters dealing with this.

Likewise, the staffing and management of a camp is a specialized consideration. Books, camping conferences, and organizations such as the Christian Camp and Conference Association provide information and helps.

Personnel

Where there is an active camping program it is usually advisable to have a camping coordinator on the board of Christian education. His duties will include such matters as coordinating camp dates with the church schedule, guiding camp promotion, recruiting necessary camp personnel, and encouraging camp follow-through.

DIRECTOR

When the church is to provide its own staff for its camp program, the first position to be filled is that of *director*. A

Christian education director, when available, would be a first choice. Other good possibilities include school recreation directors, athletic coaches, and public school teachers. Organized camping experience is a high priority in qualifications.

NON-COUNSELING STAFF

Some authorities divide camp personnel into counseling staff and non-counseling staff. The non-counseling staff members have responsibilities in such areas as health (doctor, nurse, first-aid personnel), food (dietician, cooks, kitchen and dining room help), maintenance (caretaker and assistants), and business (business manager, store manager, office personnel). This type of personnel is usually associated with an established resident camp.

COUNSELING STAFF

The counseling staff is composed of the cabin counselors and such personnel as deal directly with the campers. Often the designation "program staff" is used.

Usually one of the key tasks of the church camp is the recruitment and training of camp *counselors*. A basic ratio of counselors to campers is one counselor for each eight campers. As the person who spends the most time with the camper in the 24-hour-a-day camp experience, the counselor is often the key to the effectiveness of the camp effort. Joy MacKay in *Creative Counseling For Christian Camps* goes so far as to say that ". . . the quality of the counseling staff is much more important than the site, the facilities, and the program put together."[5]

It is generally recommended that counselors be at least 19 years of age; possess basic spiritual and emotional maturity; enjoy camp life; have good health; and get along well with people. To this might be added a sense of humor, attitude of impartiality, and a general ability to stand the stress and strains of prolonged interpersonal relationships.

Other program staff positions would be related to recreation, crafts, music, Bible study, and missions.

It should be pointed out that while there has been a division into counseling and non-counseling staffs, in actual practice the two often merge. A nurse, for example, might have one of the most effective personal work ministries in camp, even though this position is listed as non-counseling.

Program

Camp program is essentially a balanced schedule of recre-

---

[5]Joy MacKay, *Creative Counseling for Christian Camps* (Wheaton, Ill.: Scripture Press Publications, Inc., 1966), p. 7.

ational, educational, and group living activities. In the church camp these are in the spiritual perspective of Christian goals.

A sample daily schedule for a church camp is listed by MacKay as follows:

7:00 Reveille	1:45 Trading post
7:30 Flag raising	2:00 Rest hour
7:40 Quiet time	3:15 Third activity
8:00 Breakfast	4:30 Free Swim
8:30 Cabin and camp cleanup	5:45 Supper
9:00 Bible study	6:45 Evening program
10:15 First activity	9:15 Cabin call
11:30 Second activity	9:40 Cabin devotions
1:00 Dinner	10:00 Taps[6]

This schedule would vary, of course, for different age groups, but indicates the basic elements of the daily program.

A sample daily schedule for a day camp is given by Seger in *Planning a Christian Day Camp*.[7] It begins at 9:00 o'clock with staff prayer and closes with a 3:30 p.m. camper dismissal. The program includes such activities as Bible drill on nature verses, nature hunts, crafts, games, swimming, and Bible stories. Campers bring sack lunches for noon meal.

Facilities and Equipment

These will depend on the type of camping being undertaken. For any camp site development, of course, local zoning and building codes must be consulted. Many areas also have strict regulations concerning sanitary, kitchen, and sleeping facilities for camps. Local authorities should be consulted on these matters before any camping is initiated. Likewise, use of parks or recreation areas for day camps must be cleared with proper authorities.

A general rule on camping facilities and equipment is that every effort be made to take advantage of and maintain as natural an environment as possible.

Some churches with family camping and trip camping programs have invested in some basic equipment such as tents, cook stoves, cooking equipment, and possibly sleeping bags. First aid supplies are an essential for any camping project.

Financing

The major source of camp income is through camper fees. These are usually worked out on the basis of camp operating costs. However, fees are sometimes adjusted on the basis of

---

[6]*Ibid.*, p. 70.
[7]Valerie Seger, *Planning A Christian Day Camp* (Chicago: Moody Press, 1961), pp. 65 and 66.

the campers' ability to pay. In order to provide a camp experience for deserving youngsters, many churches also provide "camp scholarships," which cover all, or part, of the camp fee for those otherwise unable to attend camp. Such scholarship funds may be in the church budget, or they may be provided for by church groups or personal gifts.

One essential expense of any camping program is camper insurance. Information on recommended policies can be obtained from Christian Camp and Conference Association. The standard camp policy covers campers from the time they leave home until they return. The cost of camper insurance can be included in the fixed charges for camp and thought of the same as food and necessary equipment.

SUMMARY

Church camping offers unique opportunities in Christian education. The outdoor setting, the 24-hour-a-day living experience, and the close leader-group relationship provide means for effective spiritual teaching and decisions for Christian life and living.

Major types of camping used by churches are: resident camps, which have permanent facilities; day camps, where overnight accommodations are not involved; and trail camps, which have no regular camp site, but move from place to place with various modes of travel.

Of vital importance in the effectiveness of the camping program is the camp counselor. The close relationship to the camper makes it imperative that men and women of spiritual and emotional maturity be chosen for this responsibility.

SHARING YOUR THINKING

1. Seek to establish two outstanding values of Christian camping.
2. Into what categories can a camp staff be divided and what is the practical significance of these categories?
3. What reasons can be given for counselors to have few, if any, duties besides their counseling responsibilities?

PRACTICAL PROJECTS

1. Make a survey of a Bible book such as Genesis or Matthew and list those persons and events that might be interpreted as being related to a camping program.
2. Plan a rainy day program for camp.
3. Visit a camp in operation to study its organization and operational procedures.

RESOURCES

Bibliography

American Camping Association Standards. Martinsville, Ind.: American Camping Association.

Day Camp Standards - American Camping Association. Martinsville, Ind.: American Camping Association.

Dimock, Hedley A. (ed). **Administration of the Modern Camp.** New York: Association Press, 1948.
   This is a standard reference book on organized camping, dealing with the principles and techniques of camp administration.

Hammett, Catherine T., and Musselman, Virginia. **The Camp Program Book.** New York: Association Press, 1951.
   This is an exceptionally fine book on camp programming. It contains helpful suggestions and illustrations on a wide variety of activity.

MacKay, Joy. **Creative Counseling for Christian Camps.** Wheaton, Ill.: Scripture Press Publications, Inc., 1966.
   Here is a practical resource book for the counselor. It covers much counseling activity, but has a major section on campcraft skills.

Mattson, Lloyd D. **Camping Guideposts.** Chicago: Moody Press, 1962.
   A workbook type of publication, this is designed to be used as a training manual for the Christian counselor.

Mitchell, A. Viola, and Crawford, Ida B. **Camp Counselling.** Philadelphia: W. B. Saunders Company, 1950.
   Here is a book for the counselor who needs knowhow in various phases of camp craft and outdoor living.

Seger, Valerie. **Planning a Christian Day Camp.** Chicago: Moody Press, 1961.
   This is a paperback that touches on various aspects of working with a Christian day camp.

Todd, Floyd and Pauline. **Camping for Christian Youth.** New York: Harper & Row, 1963.
   A basic text for those engaged or interested in Christian camping, it is a good treatment of the evangelical philosophy of camping and the practices that grow out of that philosophy.

Organizations Which Help

AMERICAN CAMPING ASSOCIATION
   Bradford Woods, Martinsville, Ind. 46151

CHRISTIAN CAMP AND CONFERENCE ASSOCIATION
   P.O. Box 400, Somonauk, Ill. 60552

CHAPTER 7

Adult Fellowship

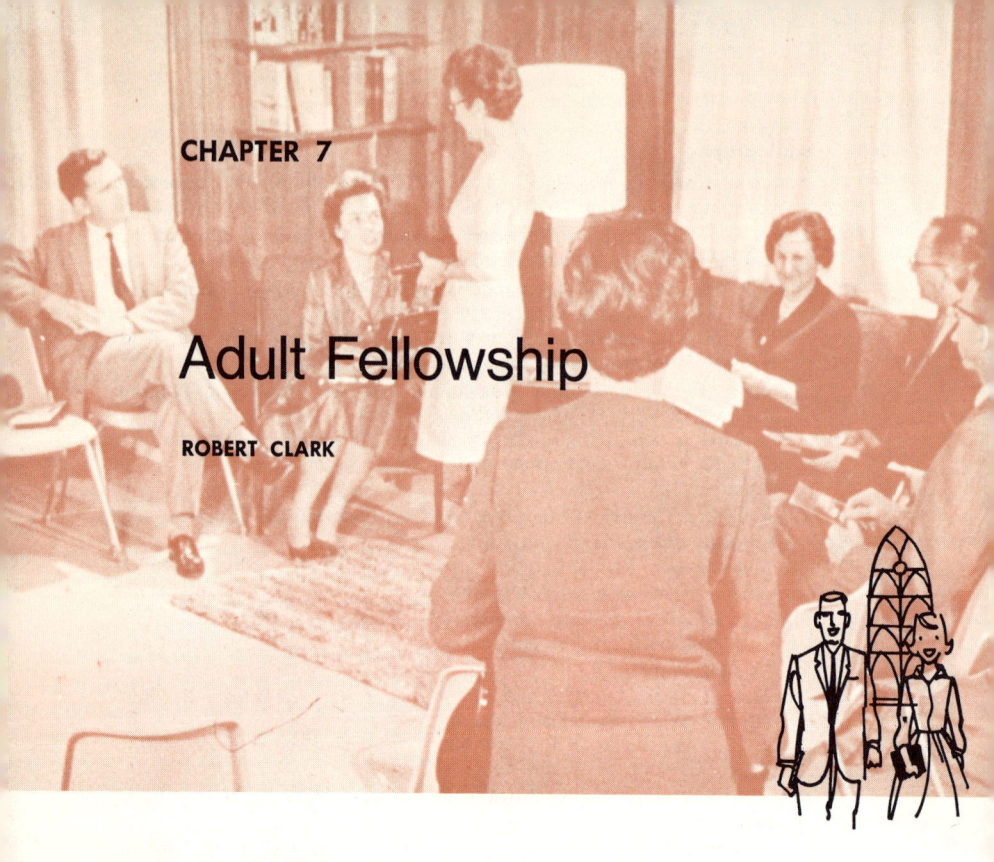

ROBERT CLARK

ASK YOURSELF

These are questions to orient preclass thinking.
They may also be used as review after study.

1. What is an adult fellowship program?
2. What are some values of adult fellowship?
3. What types of adult fellowships are there?
4. What are some differences in planning for the three major age groupings?
5. How does adult fellowship organization relate to other parts of the church program for adults?

DO YOU KNOW?

Opportunity for Christian fellowship serves a vital purpose in the church program for adults. This has been recognized by the church from earliest times. "And they, continuing daily with one accord in the temple, and breaking bread from house to house, did eat their meat with gladness and singleness of heart" (Acts 2:46).

Church fellowship can be either spontaneous or organized. As Christians meet together there is a unity of the Spirit that

---

Robert Clark., Ed.D., *Moody Bible Institute faculty*

the Apostle Paul has referred to as "the bonds of fellowship." This does not require specific meetings and exists apart from formal organization.

However, there is also a place for times of organized fellowship. Such times are important, both in giving the adults an opportunity for becoming acquainted and enjoying each other's company as fellow believers, and also as means for increasing community outreach.

What Is Adult Fellowship?

Adult fellowship is that part of the church's Christian education program that is established specifically to provide purposeful Christian fellowship and witnessing outreach for adults.

VALUES OF ADULT FELLOWSHIP PROGRAM

Adult fellowship possesses values which have a vital place in the church educational ministry.

Meets Basic Personality Needs

A fellowship program offers opportunities for the meeting of individual needs relating to not only social fellowship, but to sense of belonging, recognition, security, and similar aspects of adult personality.

Provides Service Opportunities

Outlets for Christian service are provided through fellowship, and Christian growth is encouraged.

Strengthens Total Adult Program

Fellowship activities give balance to the adult program by providing for social needs with a Christian perspective.

Reaches Unchurched

Community outreach is expanded by opportunities to invite outsiders to social activities that serve as Christian witness.

Encourages Unity

The unity of the adult membership of the church can be further strengthened by the companionship of social activity and shared service projects.

TYPES OF ADULT FELLOWSHIP PROGRAM

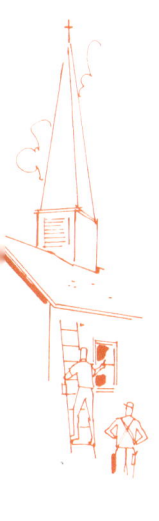

Each church must determine its own needs for adult fellowship, but outlined here are some basic patterns of organization. It is better to have a few effective organizations than to have many organizations accomplishing little.

By Age Groups

The social fellowship of many churches is closely related to the Sunday school program and usually follows the adult class divisions. The simplest division is into young adults, middle adults, and senior adults. The following chart suggests a broad age grouping, within which further divisions can be made:

Group	Age
Young Adults	25 - 40
Middle Adults	41 - 65
Senior Adults	66 and over

This chart is very flexible. Young people who marry before they are 25 years of age would be in the young adult group, and should have a married couples group as closely age grouped as possible. Age groupings generally will be guided by the needs and size of the local church.

By Sex

Many churches have separate fellowship organizations for the men and for the women. In this type of organization, the men meet together at regular intervals and usually have a basic constitution and officers to guide their activities. The women's group follows the same pattern.

The purpose of both the men's and women's fellowship organizations is to provide spiritual and social fellowship, with emphasis on appropriate service projects. Often the groups sponsor the church's boys' and girls' club programs. Both men and women may also work closely with missionary projects, and maintain special responsibilities for conducting services and witnessing in local institutions.

By Interest

There are many possibilities for adult groups based on particular areas of interest. These include such activities as athletics, hobbies, and church work projects.

Mothers with young children, as one example, have organized mothers' clubs to share together in the practical needs and problems relating to child care, and related spiritual concerns.

In all of these possibilities for interest groups there needs to be the reminder for careful evaluation of purpose and relationship to the total church program.

RELATIONSHIP TO OTHER CHURCH AGENCIES

The Sunday school provides adults with a foundation in

Bible study. There is opportunity for worship during the worship services of the church. Adult fellowship groups meet during the week and fulfill the need for fellowship and service. No single church agency can fully meet all the varied needs of the adults. However, as adult organizations work together, they can provide a balanced program to help adults become mature, well-integrated Christian personalities.

The adult fellowship groups are related to each other as well as to the total church program through the board of Christian education. As part of the board's administration, an adult council can help plan, correlate, and supervise all activities in the adult division.

ORGANIZING ADULT FELLOWSHIPS

Personnel

Fellowship groups usually elect their own leaders. These officers give direction to the organization and also serve as the planning committee. Broader involvement can also be developed by the appointment of a program committee to arrange for activities and meetings.

Program

FOR YOUNG ADULTS

Young adults are gregarious and enjoy social and service functions. However, an average young adult group may include highly companionable couples, unmarried people, and those with spouses disinterested in spiritual matters or of different faiths. Employment or family responsibilities may further affect attendance at fellowship gatherings. A young adult group must therefore plan programs with these factors in mind. Baby sitting provisions, for example, are usually an important consideration.

With the major emphasis on fellowship and service, adult fellowship program planning usually considers recreational activities, service projects, inspirational and devotional time, and refreshments. Overall planning should be made for a year and detailed plans for at least a quarter ahead. It is important that a record be kept of activities so that duplications and omissions can be avoided in future planning.

Service projects make an important contribution to the development of young adults. Working together on a worthwhile project builds both the individual and the group. Projects might include community outreach through visitation programs or sponsorship of a branch Sunday school or vacation Bible school. There could be church service projects, such as responsibility for staffing the nursery, ushering at specific times, or undertaking a renovation or refinishing project. Missionary service projects can be carried out through denominational programs or by direct relationship with a church-sponsored missionary on the field.

FOR MIDDLE ADULTS

While this group will have the same basic program aims as suggested for young adults, the program should be planned according to the specific needs and interests of middle adults. Normally this age group has children in the teen-college group and represents a more secure vocational and financial situation. There will be less interest in extremely active recreational activity and more concern for purposeful social fellowship.

FOR SENIOR ADULTS

Senior adult fellowship activities will be less strenuous and service projects will be geared to the physical and material limitations of this age group. Other factors to be considered are the added leisure time of senior adults and the continuing increase in their numbers.

Facilities

The church which has a comfortably furnished fellowship hall is well equipped for its adult fellowship program. A carpeted room furnished on the order of a large home living room is ideal for informal fellowship. Active game periods are usually held in a church gymnasium or recreation room. Where church facilities are inadequate, homes or rented facilities may have to be used.

Financing

Financial concern of adult fellowship organizations is often related to provision of refreshments. It is wise to establish and maintain a definite policy as to expenditures and method of financing. Usually this is done through the board of Christian education or its adult council, and includes policy and budgeting for all financial matters.

SUMMARY

Fellowship, social as well as spiritual, has a vital place in the life of the church. It is a bond which strengthens church relationships and increases the church witnessing outreach into the community. Adult fellowship organizations, within the broad divisions of young adult, middle adult, and senior adult, also provide opportunities for practical service projects. These include such possibilities as sponsorship of boys' and girls' clubs, missionary projects, witnessing teams, and church service activities.

SHARING YOUR THINKING

1. How can the adult organizations in your church correlate their programs for more effective outreach in the community?
2. What is a good balance of social and service activities in an adult fellowship?
3. Discuss the strengths and weaknesses of your present adult fellowship organizations and make specific suggestions for improving the weaknesses.

PRACTICAL PROJECTS

1. List the adult fellowship organizations in your church and in consultation with the leader of each group determine for what purpose each exists.
2. Make a list of potential projects for one of your adult fellowship organizations.
3. Chart how your adult fellowship organizations are related to each other and to the other agencies in the adult division of the church. What could be done to improve the relationships?
4. Outline a year's program for a young adult, middle adult, or senior adult fellowship organization.

RESOURCES

Bibliography

Caldwell, Irene. **Adults Learn and Like It.** Anderson, Ind.: Warner Press, 1961.
   Chapter three concerns the adult fellowship: dynamics, development, and elements which make for fellowship.

Culver, Elsie. **New Church Programs with the Aging.** New York: Association Press, 1961.
   Chapter six provides suggestions for fellowship times for older people in the church.

Hanson, Joseph. **Our Church Plans for Adults.** Valley Forge, Pa.: Judson Press, 1962.
   Chapter three deals with educational programs and activities. A survey of the activities is presented with practical helps in organization and administration.

Jacobsen, Henry. **How to Organize Adults.** Wheaton, Ill.: Scripture Press, 1963.
   This booklet deals with adult department and class organization. Adult class officers, committees, and promotion are discussed.

Jacobsen, Marion L. **Good Times for God's People.** Grand Rapids: Zondervan Publishing House, 1952.
   This is a book of resource material for all who need help in planning social activities.

Rismiller, Arthur. **Older Members in the Congregation.** Minneapolis: Augsburg Publishing House, 1964.
   Pages 66-96 deal with fellowship for the older person in the congregation. Benefits of a club program are suggested. Also, practical helps are given on starting, promoting and conducting a club program.

CHAPTER 8

Youth Program

GILBERT A. PETERSON

ASK YOURSELF

These are questions to orient preclass thinking.
They may also be used as review after study.

1. Why should there be a program other than Sunday school for youth in the church?
2. What are the elements in a successful leadership program for young people?
3. What type of social program should a church provide for young people?
4. How can a local church develop an effective guidance program for its youth?
5. In what ways can young people serve the Lord in and through the local church?

DO YOU KNOW?

The church youth program* is one of the church's key educational challenges. Here is opportunity to provide Chris-

---

*While everything that a church does for its young people could be included in "youth program," the term is used here to designate the expressional program usually associated with Sunday evening. The program may, of course, be held at other times than on Sunday or in the evening.

Gilbert A. Peterson, Ph.D., *Trinity Evangelical Divinity School*

tian guidance for young people during the time of some of their most crucial decisions.

It is, of course, no easy matter to reach and hold young people with an effective youth ministry. It takes thorough planning and dedicated effort.

In the planning it is well to remember that young people desire activity, and many feel the church ministry for youth is inadequate in this regard. However, it is also important that the activities be part of a balanced program and be carefully related to the church's Christian education objectives.

There now exists a larger teen-age population than ever before in our history, and educators speak of a "youth culture." The church faces the challenge of guiding this generation for the cause of Christ, and an effective youth program provides one very practical means to this end.

What Are Church Youth Programs?

Church youth programs are church-sponsored, organized activities specifically for young people, designed to provide especially leadership development and Christian fellowship.

VALUES OF YOUTH PROGRAMS

Youth programs have at least four outstanding values. (1) They provide opportunity for leadership development by opening leadership roles and guiding youth in them. (2) They encourage wholesome, satisfying social experience, which is an important part of a young person's life. Witness for Christ can also be a natural part of such experience. (3) By group and personal guidance in spiritual growth and problems, youth are helped to move from spectator to participant in their problem solving. (4) Youth programs also open doors to meaningful service for the Lord, with implications for future faithfulness.

TYPES OF YOUTH PROGRAMS

The youth program of the local church is designed to bring young people together for expressional and leadership opportunities not available in other areas of the church program.

Sunday Evening Programs

The Sunday evening program usually precedes the evening service. It is planned especially as an expression opportunity, with young people sharing in the planning, directing, and presentation of the program.

Weekday Programs

Some churches conduct youth meetings on weekday evenings. This makes possible, if desired, informal recreation or organized sports early in the evening with the more formal study program following.

RELATIONSHIP TO OTHER AGENCIES

To Agencies Within the Church

If the youth program is to be effective and productive it must (1) be distinctive in its contribution to the church program, (2) work cooperatively with the other educational agencies to provide for balanced coverage of biblical truth, Christian living, and service experiences. While the church service is basically for worship and the Sunday school for instruction, the youth program features involvement through expression and training.

To the Home

The youth program is not a substitute for the home, but rather should seek to cooperate with the home in equipping today's youth—tomorrow's homemakers—for their role of Christian leadership and mature adulthood.

ORGANIZING YOUTH PROGRAMS

Concerned and trained adult leaders
+ a group of participating young people
+ a functional organizational pattern
+ stimulating program materials
+ careful, long-range planning
+ much cooperative work
_____

= a successful youth leadership program

Personnel

Dedication to the Lord demonstrated by a vibrant Christian experience, coupled with a sincere love for young people, is essential for adult advisers of youth. Also basic are ability to adapt to changing situations, a sense of humor, patience, a willingness to sacrifice time and personal pleasures, and an ability to organize and follow through on plans and programs.[1]

Many churches are finding that the use of an advising team (preferably a married couple) has advantages over using just one adviser. This enables fellows and girls both to feel

---

[1] For a fuller description of the adult adviser's role, see chapter 2 in *How to be a Youth Sponsor* by Roy B. Zuck and Fern Robertson, (Wheaton, Ill.: Scripture Press Publications, 1960).

they have an adviser for their particular concerns. It also provides for a broader sharing of responsibilities.

Youth leadership elected by the group usually includes a president, secretary, treasurer, and social chairman. To these may be added—depending upon the size of the group—vice-president, missions chairman, visitation chairman, promotion chairman and similar positions of responsibility.

Program

PROVIDING LEADERSHIP OPPORTUNITIES

Leadership is taught by actively involving people in leading, and the concept of a laboratory situation is recommended for the youth program. Adult advisers may produce more polished and well organized meetings; however, we must decide whether we want to "put on a program" or enable young people to develop leadership skills.

THROUGH PROGRAM VARIETY

In the Sunday evening youth program there is opportunity to test and encourage the talents of youth. Such vital questions as dating, courtship, marriage, honesty, temptation, vocational choice, race relations, soul winning, and doctrine may be considered. Meaningful and honest answers will be sought by the young people through a variety of methods. These methods might include debates, panel discussions, quizzes, simulated radio and T.V. programs, drama, interviews, and demonstrations.

THROUGH PLANNING GROUPS

In order to develop leadership qualities the young people are divided into planning-program groups. The number of these groups will vary with the size of the youth work. However, the basic principle is to get as many young people to participate as possible. A youth division, whether junior high school, senior high, or college and career, should have a minimum of two groups.

This division into planning groups will provide greater involvement on the part of more young people. Adult advisers are assigned to each unit. Keeping the ratio of one adult advising team to every ten young people will make planning easier. For a group of ten or less young people, there would be one advising team, if possible, with two planning-program youth units. For a unit of twenty young people, two adult advising teams would be recommended. The young people should be divided into teams representing a balance of abilities, experience, and leadership. Tactful supervision and follow-up is the key to a leadership development program.

PROVIDING SOCIAL EXPERIENCE

Learning to live and work cooperatively is a skill all need to acquire. Just "having a party" does not provide that training. A well planned social activity usually offers some learning opportunity or means of Christian witness. While fellowship itself is a legitimate objective, alert and informed adult youth advisers can often guide into other objectives as well. A post-athletic game fellowship, for example, can be a practical means of reaching non-Christian students. A "catch-up social" where a social event is created without announcement can give guidance for good use of leisure time.

Here are some general suggestions for planning social activities:

1. Determine the social needs of the youth in your group.
2. Group the needs into major categories, relating to specific social activity.
3. List the potential social activities open to your youth.
4. Program one major and one minor social event each month.
5. Carefully plan the events with your youth.
6. Evaluate each event immediately after it has taken place.
7. Conserve tested activities. Try new ones.

GIVING GUIDANCE

Seward Hiltner writes that "The great need in work with young people today is for communication or genuine encounter or meeting between teen-agers and adults, which is at a deep rather than superficial level, and which respects rather than violates the emerging self-respect of the adolescent."[2] It is this type of honest guidance that youth seek and need in an ever changing world scene.

Here is the place for the understanding and prepared youth worker. His job is to establish a relationship of trust with the young person, listen to him, see the problem from his point of view, and offer advice, support, clarification, or just an available ear. Not too quick to advise, yet not reticent to show God's plan and answer as given in the Word of God, must be the counselor's rule.

INFORMAL COUNSELING

A workable guidance program is both planned and unplanned. Informal counseling takes place in the car as you drive along, on outings, and at athletic events when casual remarks are exchanged and attitudes displayed. Through

---

[2] Seward Hiltner, "Adolescents and Adults," *Pastoral Psychology,* December 1960.

casual conversation, before or after services or meetings, vital issues are raised in a permissive environment. Informal contacts can be the most influential factors in our work with youth.

FORMAL COUNSELING

The more formal guidance and counseling session can also be considered. One effective procedure is to announce a regular program of individual counseling which will ultimately involve your entire group. A carefully selected place is needed, and regular appointments are made. The counselor should have available a variety of printed materials on major problem areas to give out as the need arises. A simple but orderly interview agenda can be used to give direction to the session. Friendliness, concern, and sincere interest in the young person should be in abundant evidence.

It should be pointed out that the counseling referred to here concerns spiritual help, basic vocational guidance, and other areas that can be handled by a mature Christian adviser. Matters requiring professional counseling must be referred to the pastor and such professional help as may be advisable.

Youth of today are looking for adults who will demonstrate their sincerity to the Lord and to them. A dedicated and sincere personal guidance program can do much to conserve gains made in other areas of church ministry.

OPENING DOORS OF SERVICE

Opportunity for young people to put into practice that which they have been learning is also necessary. Service opportunities exist throughout the church program. Some areas in which youth can be utilized are: vacation Bible school, both as helpers and as leaders; mimeographing and mailing for the church; general ground and maintenance care; and visitation of other youth, of shut-ins, and social institutions. Other opportunities are in witnessing through missions, street meetings, or tract distribution, and participation in the church program through ushering, music, nurseries, children's church, and boys' and girls' clubs.

"Use me or lose me" has been a clarion call of youth. Provision must be made for the significant contribution that teenagers can and want to make to the total life of the church.

Facilities and Materials

Ideal facilities for youth activities include places for sports and socials, as well as a comfortable room for regular meetings. Few churches have ideal facilities, but many will find with investigation and work that suitable facilities can be arranged.

Materials are another key to a productive program. Both adult leaders and youth need to have available resource material on the relevant issues confronting Christians today. Also needed are varied and lively methods for considering the issues—methods which will produce the involvement of youth in the solutions to these problems.

When selecting program materials, keep the following guidelines in mind:

1. Are the program subjects meaningful to the young people?
2. Does the material allow for the development of a biblical answer to the problems discussed?
3. Will the materials be handled in such a way that youth will be trained in leadership skill and spiritual discernment?
4. Does the material fit into an overall plan of curriculum that will lead the young people to consider a wide range of topics in an orderly manner?
5. Do the youth program materials correlate with the materials being used in other church agencies?

Financing

Young people are often able to carry the financial responsibility of their youth program from funds given in offerings and through special youth fund-raising projects. An expanded program, however, may require supplemental financing. The church may provide a definite budget allotment for youth work, or give such help as camp "scholarships."

SUMMARY

The teen-age population is growing steadily, and the church faces an increasing challenge to provide Christian leadership development opportunities. Such programs as the traditional Sunday evening youth meetings can be used effectively for this.

The concept of a laboratory situation is especially pertinent. To provide learning opportunities, youth programming must use materials and methods that involve the young people. Subject matter must be practical and deal with their problems and needs. Biblical truths will become meaningful as they are understood in application to everyday experiences.

Adult advisers provide mature guidance for the young people and seek to encourage their Christian initiative and leadership growth. Opportunities for service are an important part of this growth, as are purposeful social experiences.

SHARING YOUR THINKING

1. Have each class member select one youth known to him, and without identifying the person, state his one greatest need. When all needs are listed, discuss the qualities needed by an adult adviser to effectively help these young people.
2. Discuss ways of implementing parent-youth communication in your church.
3. Discuss as a group of youth sponsors (actual or potential) one or two key problems to be faced in the administration of a youth program.

PRACTICAL PROJECTS

1. Visit a Sunday evening program for youth in a local church and study it from the standpoint of adult leadership, youth involvement, and program and room preparation.
2. Interview five teen-agers concerning their interest in their church's total program, specifically as to their recommendations on the youth program.
3. Chart the relationships which exist between the various parts of your church's total program for youth. Use solid lines to show what relationships do exist and broken lines to show what relationships should be added.

RESOURCES

Bibliography

Hoglund, Gunnar, and Grabill, Virginia. **Youth Leader's Handbook.** Wheaton, Ill.: Miracle Books, 1958.
   A practical "how to" booklet covering topics from youth retreats to making speeches.

Santa, George F. **Youth Leader's Handbook,** Numbers One and Two. Redondo Beach, Calif.: Christian Workers' Service Bureau, 1955.
   A helpful set of booklets dealing with the organization problems and relationships confronted by the adult worker with youth in the formulation and development of a Sunday evening youth program.

Towns, Elmer L. **Successful Youth Work.** Glendale, Calif.: Gospel Light Publications, 1966.
   A book dealing with all phases of the program for youth in the local church.

Zuck, Roy B., and Robertson, Fern. **How to be a Youth Sponsor.** Wheaton, Ill.: Scripture Press Publications, 1960.
   A booklet for adults presenting a step-by-step approach to effective work with youth groups, covering the purpose of the group, the sponsors' role, and development of the youth program.

Further Contacts

Some publishers referred to in the bibliography above also publish youth program materials. Check with your own Sunday school materials publisher. In some cases effort is made to coordinate the youth materials with the Sunday school curriculum.

CHAPTER 9

Boys' and Girls' Clubs

J. OMAR BRUBAKER

ASK YOURSELF

These are questions to orient preclass thinking.
They may also be used as review after study.

1. What is meant by church "activity programs"?
2. Why should a church provide boys' and girls' activity programs?
3. What types of club activity can be used in the church?
4. What is the relationship of a club program to the Sunday school?
5. What place will the Bible have in an activity program?
6. What does an activity program require in the way of facilities, equipment, and finances?

DO YOU KNOW?

The appeal of an activity program, usually organized as a club, brings youngsters into the church program and opens challenging doors for Christian witness, teaching, and training.

A Christ-centered boys' or girls' club basically provides a potential of several hours of Christian education influence upon impressionable lives each week. In a materialistic society, with relative moral standards and disintegrating home life,

---

J. Omar Brubaker, M.A., *Moody Bible Institute faculty*

such influence is greatly needed. Many boys and girls who are not related to any other agency of the church can be reached through activity programs, and their use in evangelical churches continues to increase.

What Are Church Boys' and Girls' Clubs?
These are church-sponsored, organized programs of wholesome recreation and achievement whose Christ-centered emphasis leads to new life and growth in Christ.

VALUES OF WEEKDAY ACTIVITY PROGRAMS

Community Outreach

"May I go to the boys' club at the church tonight?" asks the junior boy from an unchurched home. Permission being given, the boy finds activities that match his desire for action and fun. But he also senses genuine interest and friendship on the part of the club leaders, for in the type of program being discussed there would also be a sincere concern to eventually lead this junior boy into the new life that there is in the Lord Jesus Christ.

Here, then, is a youngster, with no previous relationship to church or Sunday school, being reached through a Christ-centered activity program. Not only is *he* being reached, but there is now a contact that could reach the entire family as well.

Christian Character Building

An activity program is a ministry which helps Christian boys and girls grow in the Lord. In the course of group activities they learn to practice Christian principles of behavior and develop Christian leadership. Jacobsen says,

Play is one of the Christian educator's best methods for molding character . . . The effective teacher will not fail to utilize this method of developing character—that part of personality that involves moral qualities.[1]

Desire for fun and recreation is met in a Christian atmosphere, and new skills and creative ability are developed in working with practical crafts and hobbies.

Teaching the Bible

An activity program to be worthy of a place in the church program of Christian education will in a generous measure communicate the Word of God. Materials should be Bible-based and doctrinally sound.

---

[1]Marion Jacobsen, "Recreation," *An Introduction to Evangelical Christian Education,* ed. J. Edward Hakes (Chicago: Moody Press, 1964), p. 346.

Scripture memory in a club program can be handled so that the truth is taught meaningfully and applied practically. "In the requirements which send the boy or girl into actual exploration and memorization of God's Word, there are valuable opportunities for spiritual counsel."[2] An effective program will also encourage and strengthen habits of personal Bible study and private devotions.

Spiritual Growth Through Example and Counsel

Leaders have various types of contacts with youngsters in the weekday club activities. These provide opportunity for the Christian character and example of the leaders to show through in normal, informal ways. Further, as the club members get to know their leaders, friendship and fellowship are strengthened and opportunity for spiritual counseling increases. Children and youth who have confidence in the sincerity and spirituality of their leaders freely share their problems and accept counsel.

At the same time, the leaders see the boys and girls in a natural situation. Problems come to the surface, and needs are more clearly manifested. As Jacobsen notes:

Once the learner has been brought into contact with one who is able to teach him the things of God (and this may well have been facilitated by a recreational event), play further serves this ministry by breaking down the barriers that keep people apart.[3]

Reaching the Whole Person

The church's program should be developed in terms of its ministry to persons—entire individuals. If our Christian education programs are to be adequate, they must be balanced with a proper emphasis upon instruction, worship, expression, fellowship, and service. In programs that minister to physical, social, and emotional needs, in addition to the mental and spiritual, the church is demonstrating an interest in the entire individual. A Christ-centered program will be concerned with developing well-integrated, Christian personalities. Russell notes:

Through a carefully planned weekday activity program, young people can be guided to appreciate all of life as a gift from God, and to participate in all phases of it to glorify God and enjoy Him. In developing such an attitude, there will come integration of life around the center—Christ.[4]

---

[2]Eunice Russell, "Weekday Youth Clubs," *An Introduction to Evangelical Christian Education*, ed. J. Edward Hakes (Chicago: Moody Press, 1964), p. 287.
[3]*Op. cit.*, p. 346.
[4]*Op. cit.*, p. 286.

TYPES OF ACTIVITY PROGRAMS

National Organizations

Many churches prefer to adopt a weekday activity or club program that is already clearly outlined, developed, and proven successful. Such programs are available from some denominations and from organizations whose purpose it is to serve the local church. Examples of evangelical, interdenominational programs would be: the Awana Youth Association's club programs for boys and girls, the Christian Service Brigade for boys, and Pioneer Girls for girls. Some churches have worked with the Scouting program, adding their own spiritual and Bible emphasis.

Established plans have the advantage of providing tested, well-balanced programs with the necessary materials, as well as helpful services from the sponsoring organization. The fact of belonging to a large national organization may also prove attractive to new members being recruited.

Individual Church Programs

Where a church prefers to work out its own program, this may be done in terms of a special emphasis on sports, hobbies, handcraft projects, or whatever combination of activities may be chosen. Sometimes an existing educational program, such as a Sunday school or youth group, is expanded to include regular recreational activities. This requires careful planning along with proper leadership and supervision.

RELATIONSHIP TO OTHER CHURCH AGENCIES

The weekday activity program should not duplicate or overlap the work of the other educational agencies, but should supplement them. Its unique emphasis, in terms of program elements, is not in formal instruction and worship, but in fellowship and expression. It is not a weekday Sunday school hour or church service, but rather a social, recreational, and expressional time designed to appeal to boys' and girls' interests and meet their needs.

The weekday club program should be organized and administered as a part of the total church program for children and youth. As such, it is under the supervision of the board of Christian education. Usually there are boys' work and girls' work committees with the chairmen being from the Christian education board.

Where there are organized age-group divisions (children, youth, adults), club activity would be administered within the divisional organization.

ORGANIZING WEEKDAY ACTIVITIES

Personnel

The effectiveness of a weekday activity program is closely related to the type of leadership being used. Obtaining the proper leaders is a matter of prayer, promotion, and persistence. Normally, a productive program, well publicized and prayed for in the church and manned by enthusiastic leaders, will not lack for additional leadership.

PERSONALITY

The leader who has appeal to youngsters, if not young in years, must be young at heart. He must enjoy the age group he works with and generally enjoy life and living. He must also know the characteristics of the boys or girls. In the words of Paul, he "must not strive; but be gentle unto all, . . . apt to teach, patient" (II Tim. 2:24).

SPIRITUALITY

Christian leadership requires, above all, a genuine Christian experience. Often individuals with a special interest in club activities, even though they are young in the faith, can be used as assistant leaders as they "grow in grace." Key leaders, however, should be mature Christians with a deep sense of their spiritual responsibility.

PREPARATION

The worker needs training in order to serve effectively. Weekday activity leadership usually requires special knowledge of club meetings and activities. The leader must know well the games, achievement work, and activities he leads and be able to direct the participants effectively.

Program

The most successful program will be carried on where the activities are geared to the age level. This means that there will be different programs for juniors and junior and senior highers.

Where the church is using a denominational or national interdenominational plan, the program is already established and materials available. Usually these programs include a balance of recreational activities, individual achievement work, and spiritual teaching and challenge. Club meetings are held weekly, with older boys and girls usually meeting in the evening and younger groups meeting in the afternoons or on Saturday. Outdoor activities such as hiking and camping are included in the program.

A key part of most established programs is the development of boy or girl leadership. This involves both personal achievement work and practical leadership opportunities in the meetings.

Generally, grouping by separate sexes is best for weekday activity programs. Since these activities develop ideals and standards, both groups will benefit in future coeducational activity.

Facilities and Equipment

Elaborate facilities are not necessary. However, a basic activity area is essential for a club program. Most churches have a basement area or some other room that can be adapted for activities. Some may find school or community facilities available. Storage space should be provided for game equipment and handwork or hobby supplies. For new building plans, a multi-purpose room, which can be used for a variety of functions, should be considered.

Financing

As a vital part of the total church ministry, the activity program should be included in the Christian education budget. The youngsters usually buy their own materials and uniforms. The basic investment for the church normally includes recreational equipment and initial supplies of materials.

SUMMARY

A boys' and girls' activity program helps meet basic needs in the lives of active youngsters. When properly correlated with the total church educational program, it will assist in accomplishing the basic objectives of Christian education—reaching for Christ, building up in Christ, and sending forth for Christ.

Many churches are reaping rich dividends in terms of lives reached for Christ because of their investment in a program that takes into account youth interests and needs and ministers to the total individual.

SHARING YOUR THINKING

1. List and discuss the distinctive program aspects of a boys' club, as compared to a junior boys' Sunday school class.
2. How can the weekday activity program be fully correlated with the other agencies of the Christian education program?
3. Discuss the potential for informal contact and personal counseling in a weekday club program.
4. Discuss the advantages and disadvantages of adopting an established club program as compared to designing your own.

PRACTICAL PROJECTS

1. Visit and evaluate a weekday club program in another church.
2. Write the headquarters of a boys' or girls' club organization for information concerning their program.
3. Interview several leaders in an activity program concerning their handling of the program.

RESOURCES

Bibliography

Basic Leadership Training Course. Rolling Meadows, Ill.: Awana Youth Association, 1974.
    Written for leaders of Awana programs for grades 3 through 8.

Doan, Eleanor. **Hobby Fun.** Grand Rapids: Zondervan Publishing House, 1958.
    A resource book for projects that can be used with younger age club programs.

Hakes, J. Edward (ed.). **An Introduction to Evangelical Christian Education.** Chicago: Moody Press, 1964.
    Two chapters especially: chapter 22, "Weekday Youth Clubs" and chapter 27, "Recreation."

Leading Boys in Battalion and Stockade—Leader's Manual. Wheaton, Ill.: Christian Service Brigade, 1974.
    A handbook for leaders in two of Brigade's programs for boys.

Pioneer Girls Leader's Handbook. Wheaton, Ill.: Pioneer Girls, 1975.
    Basic leader's manual for Pioneer Girls program, but also a helpful resource for all children and youth leaders.

Potpourri. Wheaton, Ill.: Pioneer Girls, 1974.
    An activity resource book useful in planning programs for children, youth, and adults.

Torchbearers. Scottdale, Pa.: Mennonite Publishing House, rev. 1973.
    Separate leader's manuals and pupil guidebooks for boys' club programs, ages 9-14.

Understanding and Reaching Boys. Wheaton, Ill.: Christian Service Brigade, 1972.
    A course designed to help Christian men relate to boys.

Wayfarers. Scottdale, Pa.: Mennonite Publishing House, rev. 1974.
    Separate leader's manuals and pupil guidebooks for girls' club programs, ages 8-14.

Organizations Which Help

AWANA YOUTH ASSOCIATION
    3215 Algonquin Rd., Rolling Meadows, Ill. 60008
CHRISTIAN SERVICE BRIGADE
    Box 150, Wheaton, Ill. 60187
PIONEER GIRLS
    Box 788, Wheaton, Ill. 60187

Each of these organizations has organizing guides and materials, as well as program helps and resources.

CHAPTER 10

Children's Church

ROBERT F. RAMEY

ASK YOURSELF

These are questions to orient preclass thinking.
They may also be used as review after study.

1. In what sense is children's church a "church"?
2. What is the purpose of children's church?
3. How does children's church relate to family worship in the church?
4. What facilities and personnel are needed for children's church?
5. What age children should attend children's church?
6. How may children's church be related to other church agencies?
7. What is the program of a children's church?

DO YOU KNOW?

Opportunity for the child to participate in worship on his own level is offered through children's church. This program has received increasing approval and use as a part of the church's Christian education ministry.

Educationally sound and spiritually profitable, children's church reaches children with the Gospel message and also provides a practical foundation for future church relationships.

Robert F. Ramey, Th.M., *Emmaus Bible School faculty*

What Is Children's Church?

Children's church is a Sunday morning church service arranged for children and designed on the level of their understanding, usually held simultaneously with the regular adult worship service or during a portion of that time.

At one time children's church services for any age group were called junior church. With the increased interest in this ministry, closer grading has developed and divisions now usually follow the Sunday school pattern. The usual groupings now are beginner church, primary church, and junior church.

Churches with sufficiently large children's groups have found separate children's choirs to be an especially attractive possibility of the children's church program. Such choirs may periodically minister in song to the adult church congregation, thus sharing the children's church ministry with the entire church.

It should be clear from this presentation that children's church is not a duplicate Sunday school hour, nor does it seek to provide merely a child care program.

VALUES OF CHILDREN'S CHURCH

Provides Children with Meaningful Worship

Children's churches are primarily designed to provide children with meaningful worship experiences. They recognize the child's level of understanding and seek to help him establish his relationship to God in prayer, music, and the Bible.

Clarifies Worship Activities

Few actions in life become significant patterns of behavior without instruction and preparation. The child's church conduct can become purely imitative and superficial. One remedy to this is children's church. Here in early, formative years, young Christians are taught by precept and practice the meaning, as well as the elements, of New Testament group worship.

Children's church is in keeping with the principle enunciated in Proverbs 22:6: "Train up a child in the way he should go: and when he is old, he will not depart from it."

Strengthens Adult Church Service

The program strengthens the adult service by providing supervision for the untended child of non-church parents. It helps the pastor in the difficult task of preaching to meet the interests and needs of people over a wide age span. It permits maximum use of space and facilities.

Develops Family Church Worship

An outstanding advantage of children's church is the contribution it can make to family worship. While children's church sometimes divides the family pew, it more frequently unites the family. Parents who previously took turns missing church rather than trying to discipline uninterested small children, can now attend church together. A well-programmed children's church provides for periodic church attendance by children with their parents. This often brings together whole families who otherwise would not attend church. Where liberty is given for parents to determine whether or not their children should attend children's church and where children periodically attend portions of the regular service with their parents, a gradual oneness of family worship is developed. When children are enrolled explanation should be given to parents explaining the purpose and program of children's church.

TYPES OF CHILDREN'S CHURCH

Held During Entire Church Service

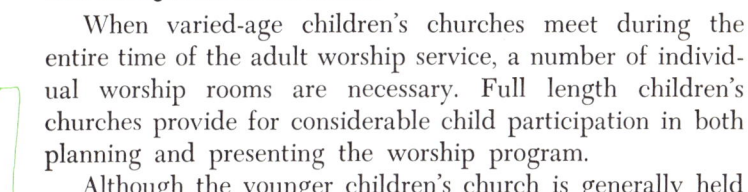

When varied-age children's churches meet during the entire time of the adult worship service, a number of individual worship rooms are necessary. Full length children's churches provide for considerable child participation in both planning and presenting the worship program.

Although the younger children's church is generally held regularly during the adult worship time, the older children sometimes participate in the regular worship service one Sunday a month. On that Sunday a children's choir can sing and the pastor can keep his young hearers in mind as he preaches.

Held During Part of the Church Service

In this plan, children are with their families or sitting together as a group during the worship service up to the time of the sermon. Then, during a hymn or other music interlude, they go to their own meeting place for the rest of the worship time.

A second variation is to have a brief children's message included in the regular service, often just before the children leave for their own activities.

Careful planning can provide for the children's church message to be on the same topic as the pastor's message, thus giving correlation of the opening program and the children's message.

Children attending the adult service without their parents are sometimes assigned to "foster parents" for the service.

Varied According to Age Groups

Children's church may be divided in a number of ways. A common age division is:

Beginner church — ages 4-5 (preschool and kindergarten)
Primary church — ages 6-8 (grades 1-3)
Junior church — ages 9-11 (grades 4-6)

The amount of a child's participation in the adult worship service can be guided by the child's ability to participate meaningfully.

RELATIONSHIP TO OTHER CHURCH ACTIVITIES

To the Church

Children's church is part of the total church program. As such, the doctrines and policies of the church are the doctrines and policies of the children's church. Church pastors are children's church pastors, although the pastor's personal participation may be limited.

To the Sunday School

Where there is close cooperation between children's church and Sunday school, the opening period of the Sunday school may be reduced in length and more time spent on the lesson. The worship service of children's church can then be a culminating experience for the children's study of the Bible in Sunday school classes.

To Other Children's Programs

Leaders of church activities for children should be aware of the other children's programs and share in the promotion. Duplication of lessons and activities should be avoided.

ORGANIZING CHILDREN'S CHURCH

Personnel

A director of children's church is normally appointed by the board of Christian education. He works with the pastor or director of Christian education in the selection of workers and general planning. Where the children's church group is divided, there may be an assistant director for each division. Each division will need a pianist who is familiar with children's songs. For children's choirs a choir director who can work with children will be needed.

Program

WORSHIP SERVICE

Leading children in worship is a challenging and profitable ministry. We are reminded that children, too, can respond to the Bible's admonition that our Heavenly Father is seeking those who will worship Him in spirit and in truth (John 4:23).

It is, of course, not possible to restrict worship to a formal service. LeBar reminds us that there is objective and subjective worship, informal and formal worship, and spontaneous or unplanned worship, and each of these types has a place in the worship activity of children.[1]

The actual formal worship service will generally follow the pattern of the adult service. There will be place for music, prayer, Scripture, offering, and sermon, with each part adapted to the age level of the group.

While this is a worship service, it must be remembered that it is *children's* worship. Not only must program activities be geared to the age level, but time schedules must also be adjusted. To keep children interested, the program must move along steadily, and sermons must be interesting and to the point, often in story form. A "heavy" program can defeat the whole purpose of this effort.

ACTIVITY PERIOD

Most children's church programs include activities other than those related directly to worship. For junior and primary churches these may constitute a separate part of the children's church session. In beginner church the activities are interwoven in the total program.

Doan and Blankenbaker refer to such a period as "Learning and Doing Time."[2] It includes activities such as learning new songs (often illustrated), Bible memorization, Bible quizzes, and missionary projects.

CHILDREN'S PARTICIPATION

Children's church offers many opportunities for children to share in the program. Often these are also opportunities to teach the meaning of church activities. Handling the offering, serving as ushers, singing in the choir, leading in prayer, and similar activities give the alert children's church director practical teaching occasions. Many junior church programs are led almost totally by the juniors themselves, under adult guidance. Participation can include a junior church board and junior minister who plan and conduct the activities.

Facilities and Equipment

Room and equipment should be conducive to quietness and reverence. The room should be light, airy, and remote enough from the sanctuary to prevent the passage of sound to and

---

[1] Lois E. LeBar, *Children in the Bible School* (Westwood, N.J.: Fleming H. Revell, 1952), pp. 301, 302.
[2] Eleanor Doan and Frances Blankenbaker, *How to Plan and Conduct a Primary Church* (Grand Rapids, Mich.: Zondervan Publishing House, 1954).

from the adult service. If the space is a Sunday school assembly area, a person must be appointed to rearrange the room quickly and neatly for the children's church. Proper size chairs should be used. Besides piano and songbooks, a worship center with pulpit or table, offering plates, choir robes, ushers' badges, and audiovisual equipment are desirable.

Financing

Expenses for a children's church program might include cost of songbooks, offering trays, weekly bulletins, and choir equipment. Normally such expenses are included in the church's Christian education budget. Children's offerings can be used to teach church stewardship, as well as missionary giving.

SUMMARY

Children's church is designed to help children have a meaningful worship experience. It is conducted specifically for children and offers them an opportunity for participation in church activity on their level of understanding.

Activity is usually graded into beginner, primary, and junior churches, following the Sunday school pattern. Programs include worship and other activity, all designed to provide an experience that will bring the child into a closer relationship to God.

SHARING YOUR THINKING

1. What scriptural support is there for children's church?
2. What should be the step-by-step advance preparation for the starting of a children's church?
3. How can music, prayer, Scripture, and stewardship be made worship experiences in children's church?
4. How may children be encouraged to participate in the planning of children's church?
5. How can Sunday school pupils be encouraged to stay for children's church?
6. How can children's church affect the daily life of the child?

PRACTICAL PROJECTS

1. Plan a children's church calendar with monthly themes for one year.
2. Develop a complete children's church service for a special day such as Christmas, Easter or Thanksgiving.
3. Assemble a display of pictures, articles, pamphlets, books, and free samples of published materials dealing with children's church.

4. Organize an observation trip to some nearby, well organized children's church program.

RESOURCES

Bibliography

Doan, Eleanor. **How to Plan and Conduct a Junior Church.** Grand Rapids: Zondervan Publishing House, 1954.
   Twelve chapters dealing with every aspect of junior church; seven completely planned programs; good bibliography.

Doan, Eleanor, and Blankenbaker, Frances. **How to Plan and Conduct a Primary Church.** Grand Rapids: Zondervan Publishing House, 1954.
   Covers all areas of primary church and has a resourse listing. Also has a section concerning kindergarten church.

Gibbs, Alfred P. **Worship: The Christian's Highest Occupation.** Fort Dodge, Ia.: Walterick, n. d.
   An unsurpassed study from Scripture of a much misunderstood concept.

Gorman, Julia A. **Church-time for Juniors.** Wheaton, Ill.: Scripture Press Foundation, 1960.
   A brief (40-page) survey of the major considerations in a junior church program.

Guide to an Effective Children's Church. Springfield, Mo.: Assemblies of God, n. d.
   An excellent 14-page booklet giving essential information and list of materials.

LeBar, Lois E. **Children in the Bible School.** Westwood, N.J.: Fleming H. Revell, 1952.
   A classic on the HOW of Christian Education; Sections C and D particularly pertinent for this study; lengthy bibliography.

Materials

Many Sunday school materials publishers now have program material available for children's church.

CHAPTER 11

Missionary Education

F. IONE ANDERSON

ASK YOURSELF

These are questions to orient preclass thinking.
They may also be used as review after study.

1. What is church missionary education?
2. Who should be responsible for church missionary education?
3. How can the Sunday school participate in missionary education?
4. What is the relationship of missionary education organization to the church missionary committee?
5. How can young people share in the church missionary convention?
6. What organization is needed for organizing a church program of missionary education?

DO YOU KNOW?

Missionary messages and budgets are accepted parts of most missionary programs. However, there is another area of missionary activity that should be a vital part of every church's ministry. This is a program of missionary education that begins with children and uses the educational agencies of the church to teach all age levels. It involves knowledge and personal involvement.

F. Ione Anderson, M.A., *formerly Canadian Bible College faculty*

What Is Missionary Education?

Missionary education is a graded approach to missions, using church educational agencies to channel missionary information and stimulate personal concern for the spread of the Gospel everywhere.

VALUES OF ORGANIZED MISSIONARY EDUCATION

The values can be summarized under three main headings.

Provides for Definite Teaching

Because it considers itself missionary-minded, a church may assume that it is teaching missions in its Sunday school and other educational agencies. Actually, there may be very little specific teaching. One of the important values of an organized program is that it enables the church to be definite about its missionary education.

Provides for Coordinated Teaching

Where the missions program is carefully planned it is possible to make the fullest use of every missionary opportunity. Speakers, conventions, and lessons will be part of a total missionary program.

Provides for Graded Teaching

Planned use of the various age group agencies permits missions teaching to be geared to definite ages. This brings missions to the level of the pupil's understanding and allows for presentations that are meaningful to him.

TYPES OF MISSIONARY EDUCATION ORGANIZATION

How the program is organized will depend in part on the size of the church. Regardless of the type of organization, however, one goal will be to involve as many of the church's educational agencies as possible.

Through the Missionary Education Committee

In a smaller church this committee may consist of only one member of the board of Christian education who is assigned the missionary education responsibility. It may also be a fuller committee.

The missionary education committee has as its chief function encouraging and developing missionary interest among all church agencies and on all age levels. It should determine what kind of missionary education is best carried out in each agency.

Through Age Group Committees

This is a further extension of the board of Christian education sub-committee idea as indicated above. Normally this means assigning the responsibility for missionary education to the established children, youth, and adult division leaders or committees.

Through the Missionary Convention

The yearly missionary convention, especially if it is well organized, offers another means of coordinating missionary education. Every member of the church from beginner on up can feel that it is his convention, and participate in it. A year-around program of planned teaching and activities should then be related to the convention.

RELATIONSHIP TO OTHER CHURCH AGENCIES

It is important to recognize that a missionary education program does not replace the church's established missionary planning channels. The planning for budgets, speakers, conventions, and similar details is the responsibility of the regular church missions committee. The board of Christian education program builds upon these plans and uses them for an effective missionary education ministry.

Coordination of planning, of course, is vital. The missionary education program is under the board of Christian education, and thus related to the total church ministry. Often the missionary education representative serves with the church missions committee.

ORGANIZING FOR MISSIONARY EDUCATION

Personnel

Regardless of the size or organization of the church, effective missionary education requires dedicated leadership. It is important to choose individuals for this responsibility who have a personal interest in missions.

MISSIONARY EDUCATION COORDINATOR

Usually this person is a member of the board of Christian education. Where there is no board, he may be appointed as the church's missionary committee representative for this responsibility.

His work will be to keep in touch with all of the church agencies and encourage knowledge and involvement in missions. He will help assign missionary speakers and projects in a coordinated schedule.

MISSIONARY EDUCATION COMMITTEE

Such a committee consists of members with specific duties:
- Chairman (or coordinator). To direct and promote the program, working with the other church agencies.
- Missionary Librarian. To be responsible for the cataloging and distribution of materials in the missionary files. Works in close cooperation with the church librarian in promotion and circulation of missionary books.
- Secretary. To keep a complete record of the missionary education program for each year and to carry on necessary correspondence.[1]

Program

THROUGH CHURCH AGENCIES

Midweek Prayer Service

The midweek service offers a practical opportunity for missionary education. The pastor may invite the missionary education committee to provide material regularly for prayer emphasis. The following are promotion suggestions: a missionary bulletin board changed weekly and placed at the entrance to the prayer room; mission prayer requests mimeographed and distributed; different people assigned fields to study and present.

Sunday School

Monthly Departmental Worship Services on Missions

The committee can help each department with resources and program ideas on the field of the month. Many students should be used in these programs, providing personal involvement.

Presession Activities

Projects for missionary education can continue from week to week prior to the Sunday school sessions. Scrapbooks may be made for mission hospitals, magazine pictures cut and mounted for the church library files, murals prepared for missionary Sunday, skits practiced, or prayer requests written out for class use.

Missionary Class Meetings

Classes may meet monthly or quarterly at church or in homes to carry out missionary projects. Some may form study and prayer groups, each having one missionary family as its responsibility.

---

[1]Mavis L. Weidman, *World Missions Folio* (Harrisburg: Christian Publications, 1960), p. A3.

Age Group Projects

These are related to a certain age person on the missionary field. Thus, a primary department may collect money to buy a dress for a primary girl on the field; a beginner department may buy shoes for a beginner child. These can be brought to the department and wrapped and mailed by the whole group.

It is important that all such projects be cleared for correct size, suitability, and similar details.

Youth Group

The person on the missionary education committee responsible for youth, together with the youth sponsor and the youth officer chosen for missionary activities, can work out a long-range program as part of the regular youth program planning.

This can include programs on the meaning and application of "missionary" witnessing by the young people; study of mission fields and problems; actual missionary experience; contact and interaction with missionaries.

Here again the missionary education coordinator will be concerned to coordinate all such planning with what is being done in the other church agencies, such as the Sunday school. The emphasis in the youth program will be toward expressional opportunities.

Clubs

Boys' and girls' weekday clubs may do craft work related to missions. Girls may make a set of missionary convention flags of the nations for a sewing badge; boys may construct models of mission stations. They may write letters to foreign children their age, and to missionaries' children. Clubs should have opportunity to choose projects and do planning on how they will achieve their goals.

THROUGH THE CHURCH MISSIONARY CONVENTION

The church missionary convention should include participation by all age groups and each church educational agency. One period of the convention may use key leaders of each agency in the church to report on their particular agency's missionary activities. These are suggestions on participation by age groups:

Involving Adults

Adult Sunday school classes, missionary societies, and fellowship organizations can be given specific adult responsibilities. Such activities might include special reports on the fields represented, conducting missionary prayer meetings, entertainment of missionaries, and preparing displays.

Involving Youth

The great potential of youth should be used to its fullest extent. They may be given responsibility for directing one convention service. They can investigate the fields represented and have a panel ready to interview the missionary. They may have charge of ushering, provide special music, or be the choir for certain nights.

Involving Children

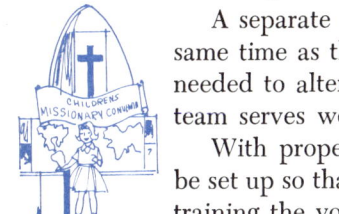

A separate children's convention may be conducted at the same time as the adult services. At least two missionaries are needed to alternate in the two services. A husband and wife team serves well.

With proper adult supervision, children's committees can be set up so that the children's convention becomes a means of training the young for leadership. Committees could include: publicity (have a poster contest), room arrangements and decorating, program, ushers, prayer meetings, finance.

Where the children will be meeting with the adults, they can share in working on such things as decorations, displays, and mailing announcements. One night may be designated as Sunday school night when teachers sit with their classes; another can be club night with boys and girls used as ushers.

Facilities and Equipment

Missionary education can utilize all of the church's educational equipment. Special missionary supplies include:

Literature, such as missionary study books, biographies, novels, magazine articles, and pictures.

Visuals, such as maps on which name tags can be pinned, globes, flannelgraph or flashcard pictures for missionary stories, filmstrips of missionary life and challenge, and flags of all countries.

Audios, such as records and tapes about missions and from missionaries.

In addition, handwork, such as murals, models, puppets, and diorama, can be utilized for missionary education.

Normally, materials for missionary education should be located and issued from the church library.

Financing

The church budget for missionary activity or for Christian education should include costs of operating a program of missionary education. If sufficient funds are provided in budget allotments all offerings received for missions during a convention can be released for direct missionary activity.

SUMMARY

Missionary education seeks to stimulate personal concern for the spread of the Gospel everywhere. It does this through the church's educational agencies, using a graded program of activities and materials.

A key place in a successful program is held by the missionary education coordinator, who usually is a member of the board of Christian education. He may have a committee working with him. His major responsibility is to work with the various church agencies, such as the Sunday school and youth groups, in setting up a definite program of missionary teaching and involvement.

For many churches the climax of their missionary program is the yearly missionary convention. With an organized missionary education ministry, the convention should involve the entire church and have meaning for every age group. The stimulus received from a convention will be reflected in the missionary program throughout the following year.

SHARING YOUR THINKING

1. Discuss the implications of the statement, "Missionary education is more than just giving facts about a foreign field."
2. Discuss ways in which the midweek prayer service could encourage missionary interest in the personal prayer life of the people.
3. Consider what your church could do to reach the home mission field (your community) in ways not being utilized at present.

PRACTICAL PROJECTS

1. Appoint a committee to investigate and list the materials for missionary education that are now available in your church.
2. Compose a questionnaire on missionary education activity to be given to each educational agency of your church to determine the interest and needs in missions study.
3. Plan at least three things your church might do to improve its missionary education program.

RESOURCES

Bibliography

Cook, Harold R. **An Introduction to the Study of Christian Missions.** Chicago: Moody Press, 1954.
    A background study book on the biblical basis and current principles in missionary work, with material on church missionary programs.

Gilleo, Alma. **How to Teach Missions.** Elgin, Ill.: David C. Cook Publishing Co., 1964.
    A small booklet which has a number of brief, practical suggestions for missions emphasis in the local church.

Hillis, Don W. **Missions for Juniors** and **Teens for Missions.** Redondo Beach, Calif.: Christian Workers' Service Bureau.
    A two-book series, the first being an introduction to missions in 12 story lessons for juniors, and the second being a 24-lesson study course for teens.

Pearson, Dick: **Missionary Education Helps for the Local Church.** Palo Alto, Calif.: Overseas Crusades, Inc., 1966.
    An excellent book of practical suggestions and available resources for missionary education.

Weiss, G. Christian. **The Bible and World Missions.** Lincoln, Neb.: Back to the Bible Broadcast, 1961.
    A correspondence school course of fourteen lessons for home study that can also be used by an adult class.

Woodward, David Brainard. **God, Men and Missions.** Glendale, Calif.: Gospel Light Press.
    This is a 13-lesson quarterly for the adult age level, with quarterlies for both teachers and students.

Organizations Which Help

Your denominational headquarters

Missionary agencies whose missionaries your church supports

Interdenominational groups as:
    INTERDENOMINATIONAL FOREIGN MISSION ASSOCIATION
    Box 395, Wheaton, Ill. 60187
    EVANGELICAL FOREIGN MISSIONS ASSOCIATION
    1405 G St., N.W., Washington, D.C. 20005

CHAPTER 12

The Board of Christian Education

EDWARD L. HAYES

Church Education

ASK YOURSELF
These are questions to orient preclass thinking.
They may also be used as review after study.

1. Why is a board of Christian education important in the church's ministry?
2. What type of boards are being used?
3. What are the steps in organizing a new board?
4. What are the major duties of a Christian education board?
5. On what basis are board members chosen?

DO YOU KNOW?

As they are put to use in the local church, the educational agencies that have been presented in this text can become a confusing schedule of unrelated activities. Or they can become a coordinated educational ministry. Usually the key to the difference is a board of Christian education (also referred to as committee or commission).

The implementation of the biblical ideal of a teaching church calls for regular planning, workable organization, adequate administration, and clear statements of policy. Creating

---

Edward L. Hayes, Ph.D., *Conservative Baptist Theological Seminary faculty*

and maintaining a board of Christian education is a practical way of accomplishing these objectives.

Failure to adequately provide for coordination can weaken the entire church ministry. Educational agencies such as the Sunday school and evening youth groups sometimes tend to operate in isolation. Competition for leadership, finances, and loyalties of the people may also develop and it is true that a program that is allowed to grow without design and purpose will have little basis for evaluation. The inadequate means of judging the success of an endeavor by counting people and their offerings is readily recognized.

What is a Board of Christian Education?

A board of Christian education is a body of church leaders elected or appointed to coordinate and guide the educational program of a church.

As the church assigns responsibility for worship and service, and delegates the management of property and finances, so the teaching program is commissioned to a board of Christian education. The general purposes of the board are (1) to establish and clarify the educational goals, (2) to unify the educational program, (3) to improve the educational outcomes, (4) to extend its educational ministry, and (5) to vitalize the spiritual impact.

VALUES OF A BOARD OF CHRISTIAN EDUCATION

Unifies the Program of Education

A board becomes a means whereby the various educational activities of the church may be fitted into a unified whole. Overlapping of purpose and function are avoided, and a balanced program can be developed.

Lends Authority to Leaders

With a board, decisions and programs need not be the responsibility of any one individual. Actions affecting policy and procedures can be handled by a board after full study and consultation. New programs are more likely to be accepted by the church if approved by a board.

Provides Continuity of Leadership

An active board provides the means for anticipating leadership needs and filling these needs. Education, by its very nature, is a continuous, ongoing ministry and should never be dependent only upon the tenure of persons in charge.

TYPES OF CHRISTIAN EDUCATION BOARDS
Representative
The council type or representative board is composed entirely of people who serve by virtue of position in the educational program. That is, they "represent" specific areas, such as the Sunday school or youth program. Many feel that the people who superintend educational agencies ought to have a direct voice in policy making. Board membership may vary from three or four to as many as nine or ten, depending upon the size of the program.

Elected
A second type is the elected board composed entirely of people selected for their broad interest in Christian education. The major responsibility of setting policy, it is contended by those who favor this type of board, calls for objective leadership. Often those closest to direct leadership are not as able as others to evaluate their work and reach decisions affecting the total scope of ministry. Such a board does not act in isolation from leaders of groups but thoroughly studies all issues, talks to all concerned, and then makes decisions in the light of their investigations.

Combination
A third type of board combines the values of the first two. Many churches create a board composed of individuals elected at large by the church, as well as representative members who serve on the board by virtue of position. This type of board assures a healthy balance between direct representation and church-wide concern.

RELATIONSHIP TO CHURCH BOARD AND LEADERS
Church Board
Usually the Christian education board is elected by the congregation and is accountable to it. Some churches deem it wise to have the Christian education board work closely with the official church board. Such a relationship may be achieved in several ways. A church board member may serve on the Christian education board as a representative. A church board member may chair the Christian education board. Regular reports may be made to the official church board. Other churches discover a suitable arrangement to be a division of responsibility among several boards. In this case the board of Christian education would have its duties clearly defined within the church constitution and would operate accordingly, accountable to the congregation.

Leaders

The relationship of the board to the pastor of the church needs to be clearly stated. The pastor is an *ex-officio* member of the board. He should be welcome at all meetings. Where there is no director of Christian education, the pastor should take an active part in guiding the activities of the board.

The relationship to a director of Christian education also needs to be established. He, like the pastor, is an *ex-officio* member of the board. His training places him in the role of an adviser of the board, and he is responsible for the implementation of board actions. As an employed staff member of the church he works with all groups and educational leaders, directing the educational ministry of the church. For long-range effectiveness it is generally best if the director does not serve as chairman of the board.

The Sunday school superintendent has a vital relationship to the board. Sunday school affairs are a major concern of the group and it may be advisable to have the superintendent serve on the board by virtue of his position. The same may be true of the director of the evening training hour or coordinator of evening youth groups.

ORGANIZING A BOARD

There are four basic steps in organizing a new board of Christian education:

1. Determine the areas of responsibility of the board in relationship to the official church board and congregation.

2. Determine board size and type of membership, taking into consideration qualifications and method of selection of members.

3. Secure church action. This may call for constitutional action.

4. Select the members as determined, and plan for initial meetings and agendas.

Personnel

Members are to be elected from the congregation for a specified time of service. Revolving terms of one to two years will assure continuity of the board. The pastor, director of Christian education, and perhaps the Sunday school superintendent and training hour director serve on the board in an *ex-officio* capacity.

Members are to be chosen for their interest in and understanding of Christian education, as well as for their knowledge of a particular phase of the church's educational program.

Much of the responsibility for an effectively functioning board rests with the chairman. The duties of the chairman include the following:

1. Arrange for and conduct the regular meetings of the board. Monthly meetings are usually necessary.

2. Appoint any subcommittees that may be needed to fulfill the objectives of the board.

3. Prepare an agenda for each meeting in cooperation with the director of Christian education.

4. Make all necessary reports to the church.

Duties

The responsibilities of a Christian education board normally include the following:

SURVEY CHURCH EDUCATIONAL NEEDS

The board should periodically make a careful survey of the educational program, facilities, equipment, budget, leadership, and curriculum to discover strengths and weaknesses. The board can follow up such a survey with positive steps to strengthen weaknesses.

ESTABLISH OBJECTIVES

Clear-cut objectives, or goals, encourage accomplishment. The board will assist groups in defining objectives and developing programs to meet them. It will seek to keep the entire educational program established on the Word of God.

APPROVE THE CURRICULUM

The board, through consultation with group leaders, approves all curriculums for use in the church. Where a published curriculum is unavailable, guidelines should be established for the creative work of group leaders.

SELECT EDUCATIONAL PERSONNEL

Careful survey of workers needed, listing of available workers, setting of standards for workers, developing a plan for recruitment, and approving workers are all major duties of the board.

TRAIN LEADERSHIP

An adequate and continuous program of teacher and leader education will be a major concern of the board. This could include a standard of certification for all teachers and workers in the church educational ministry.

RECOMMEND FINANCIAL POLICIES AND ADMINISTER THE EDUCATIONAL BUDGET

Working closely with the church finance committee or board of trustees, the board is responsible for the adequate

budgeting of funds for Christian education.

PROVIDE ADEQUATE FACILITIES, AND EQUIPMENT

The board should arrange for good teaching and learning conditions, assign space, and recommend purchase of necessary equipment and furnishings.

PROMOTE EDUCATIONAL AWARENESS

The board should seek to foster educational awareness and understanding in the congregation. Many methods may be employed, such as displays, open house for parents, and reports to the congregation.

COORDINATE ALL EDUCATIONAL WORK

As program leaders supervise and administer the work, the board receives regular reports and observes programs in action. It will serve as a clearing house for schedules and activities, seeking to keep the total program coordinated.

Dividing Responsibilities

There are three basic ways of organizing the membership of the board. The first is to divide the membership of the board into functional groupings. That is, each member is assigned to concentrate his effort in one of the following major areas: leadership education, missionary and stewardship education, curriculum, library, equipment and facilities, family life education, or weekday education. An organizational plan might look like this, with each area representing a subcommittee or individual, depending on board size:

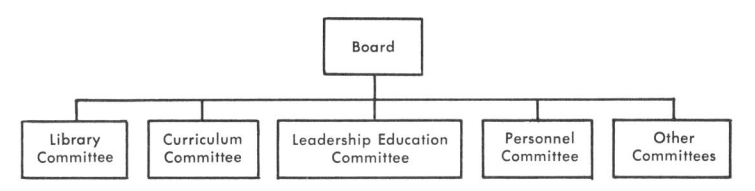

```
                          Board
    ┌──────────┬──────────┼──────────┬──────────┐
 Library   Curriculum  Leadership  Personnel   Other
Committee  Committee   Education   Committee  Committees
                       Committee
```

A second way to enlist the energies of every board member is to divide into subcommittees according to age-group interest. Members may be assigned to one of three levels of age interest: children, youth, or adults. The special areas mentioned above would then be the concern of the entire board. An organizational plan might look like this:

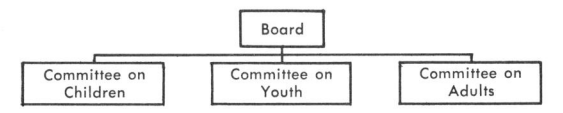

```
              Board
    ┌───────────┼───────────┐
Committee on  Committee on  Committee on
  Children       Youth         Adults
```

The third way to organize the board is to work a combination of the above two plans. It will be remembered that the purpose of delegating responsibility within the board is to develop a functional board which works with all phases of education in the church.

SUMMARY

The board of Christian education gives unified direction to the educational ministries of the church. It guards against competition for leadership, finances, and loyalties among the various agencies, as well as evaluating progress and problems.

Boards may be of a council type, where members represent particular agencies; or they may be of an elected type, where members are chosen at large. Many churches use a combination of the two types.

Among the major responsibilities of the board are the establishment of the church's educational policies and the recruitment and training of leadership.

SHARING YOUR THINKING

1. Discuss the type of board that would be best suited for your church.
2. Discuss the relationship of the pastor, director of Christian education, and Sunday school superintendent to the board.
3. How could a board in your church promote educational awareness?

PRACTICAL PROJECTS

1. Write up a description of a board and its duties for inclusion in a church constitution.
2. Visit several churches which have boards and report on how the boards are organized. If possible, attend a meeting of a board and write a summary of the activities.
3. Outline sample agendas for the first three meetings of a board in a newly organized church.

RESOURCES

Bibliography

Byrne, H. W. **Christian Education for the Local Church.** Grand Rapids: Zondervan Pub. House, 1963.

Dalton, Dean A. "The Board of Christian Education," **An Introduction to Evangelical Christian Education,** J. Edward Hakes (ed.). Chicago: Moody Press, 1964.

Gilbert, Clarence B. **The Board of Christian Education at Work.** Valley Forge, Pa.: The Judson Press, 1962.